Richard Bertinet

CRUMB

show the dough who's boss

Photography by Jean Cazals
Kyle Books

For all of the customers at the cookery school over the last 13 years who have helped to inform my teaching and my writing and who have been part of the journey, thank you.

An Hachette UK Company
www.hachette.co.uk

This edition published 2019, first published in Great Britain in 2019 by
Kyle Books, an imprint of Kyle Cathie Ltd
Carmelite House
50 Victoria Embankment
London EC4Y 0DZ
www.kylebooks.co.uk

ISBN: 978 0 85783 554 3

Text copyright 2019 © Richard Bertinet
Photographs copyright 2019 © Jean Cazals
Design and layout copyright 2019 © Kyle Cathie Ltd

Distributed in the US by Hachette Book Group, 1290 Avenue of the Americas,
4th and 5th Floors, New York, NY 10104
Distributed in Canada by Canadian Manda Group, 664 Annette St., Toronto, Ontario,
Canada M6S 2C8

To watch videos of recipes and techniques visit www.bertinet.com or www.youtube.com.

Project editor: Kyle Cathie
Design: Tina Smith Hobson
Photography: Jean Cazals
Portrait of Richard Bertinet (page 5): Dimitri Whitaker
Props styling: Tabitha Hawkins
Production: Gemma John and Nic Jones

Printed and bound in China

10 9 8 7 6 5 4 3 2

Breadboard images, by kind permission of the Antique Breadboard Museum, London:

p5 | Queen Elizabeth II's Coronation breadboard, dated 1953, made from sycamore by Bramhall, Sheffield; English oak-handled breadknife with silver enrichments and Sheffield blade.

p7 | Harvest breadboard with deeply carved wheat sprays on a wide border; breadknife with wheat and flowers, made for London ironmonger Benham of Wigmore St.

p31 | "Eat and Be Merry" board with Tunbridge ware parquetry, inscribed "Lizzie" on reverse; breadknife with spiral reeded boxwood handle and steel blade by Wade Wingfield & Rowbotham, Sheffield.

p55 | Oak presentation board carved with oak sprigs and armorials, given to the Bishop of Beverley, Yorkshire, 1891;

silver-handled breadknife, the three wheat sheaves a copy of an eighteenth-century pattern denoting support for George III against the Prince of Wales, made for London retailer Oetzmann & Co in 1903.

p111 | Serpentine-shaped oak breadboard, in the Renaissance style; "Pain" breadknife with boxwood handle, made for the French market; with a steel blade by Joseph Haywood, Sheffield.

p187 | Charming wedding board with the couple's initials in the central cartouche; breadknife with sweetcorn handle in boxwood, designed by John Bell, c. 1860, steel blade by Joseph Rodgers & Sons, Sheffield.

p207 | Harvest board with wheat, barley, oats, and rye. Late 1800s, by George Wing; continental breadknife in turned and carved oak, steel blade by Leistner.

Contents

Foreword

Bread. A staple of the human diet for centuries. The foundation of any good meal. Eaten and enjoyed the world over. How is it then that really good bread is something very hard to find?

In this book, my friend Richard Bertinet, chef and baker extraordinaire, reveals the secrets of making bread to be proud of. There are recipes galore together with hints and tips to aid your breadmaking and clear pictures showing exactly what each stage should look like.

Over time, Richard has taught me so much about making decent bread. Now, Richard's unique insight into the world of bread, formed from years of experience both of making, and in teaching people to make bread, is set down here for you too. His advice is a revelation from someone whose passion for breadmaking is unrivalled. Instead of the expected ingredients and utensils, Richard begins by saying that what is needed to make bread are "your hands, your instincts and patience" and not to look at the dough but to "feel how it responds." Richard's respect for his art and his desire to dispel the myths surrounding breadmaking is evident in his advice, which is down-to-earth, practical and invaluable to anyone who wants to bake amazing bread.

Throughout *Crumb*, Richard takes you on a fascinating journey through the history, science and methodology of breadmaking, culminating in a comprehensive collection of recipes from the traditional to the modern and for every occasion.

If you only have one book about how to make bread, this really should be it. Mind you, one word of warning! Leafing through the book will make you hungry—so get baking!

Nathan Outlaw, Michelin-starred chef and restaurateur

First

Great bread is all about the quality of the dough, the crust, and the "crumb"—the appearance and texture that epitomises a particular style of loaf. When I published my first book, *Dough*, in 2005, I just wanted to demonstrate the fun and satisfaction of combining flour, yeast, water, and a little salt into a simple, silky, and responsive dough, and to share my particular technique of working it, which is different from the more traditional English method of kneading and knocking back.

My second book, *Crust*, aimed to take the journey a stage further, with slightly more complex doughs and techniques, focusing on the role that a fantastic crust plays in the enjoyment of many styles of bread.

In the decade since then, there has been an explosion of baking books and blogs, new ideas, and different techniques. At the beginning of classes, to break the ice, I always ask my students to talk about their experiences of buying and eating bread, and why they want to make it themselves. Invariably newcomers to baking say they want to eat "clean" bread, free from additives, or they hope that baking will be a therapeutic, relaxing escape from everyday stresses. Above all, they want to learn how to make sourdough, which has become the holy grail of all bread. Then there are those who have just been given a voucher for one of my classes as a birthday present, and have no idea what they are letting themselves in for! But of those who have either had a couple of goes at making bread or have been baking for years, once we get talking, what people tell me they most want to achieve, but often struggle with, is bread with a beautifully light crumb.

No one ever says: "I'd love to make a loaf that is really heavy and dense!" When I ask them to describe their results so far, they frequently say that the texture of their bread is too tight, too doughy, or gray-looking. And when this happens repeatedly, and they don't know why, it is easy to lose confidence and become disheartened.

So this new book is all about texture. The breads I have included all have a different character, and their crumb varies from open and airy to more compact, but even a 100 percent rye sourdough that is meant to be dense should not be tight and dry. I will introduce you to some simple "soakers," ferments, and enrichments that will enhance both the texture and flavor of any bread (more about these on page 59), and I have adapted many of the recipes to work easily in a food mixer. But I want to begin, as I always do in classes, by introducing you to the way I mix and work the dough by hand, in order to really feel how magical it is when the dough comes alive. It is only when you understand the whole process, that you can become comfortable with using a mixer, and it is only when you have mastered a simple dough, that you can have the confidence to move on to more complex ferments and sourdoughs.

Tools

Your three most important tools are free: your hands, your instincts and patience. The key to great bread with a fantastic crumb is learning to touch, feel, and handle the dough with confidence. I encourage people to start off by not even looking at the dough when they are working it, but to study a picture on the wall, or to gaze out of the window; to look anywhere but at the dough itself, so they focus on really feeling the way it is responding. One of my most special moments was teaching a tiny girl who was almost blind to make bread. It was unbelievable how brilliant she was, because her hands became her eyes. She grasped the technique, and just allowed the magic to begin.

Once you master my technique, you will find that the dough is very responsive and forgiving. When you are making bread using yeast, you are harnessing something reactive that grows, changes, and responds to the conditions in which it finds itself. The more you bake, the more you will discover that your dough behaves a little differently according to the weather and temperature. In the summer, if it is very hot and dry in the kitchen, the dough might need a little more cold water, and because it will want to grow more quickly, it may need shorter resting and rising times. In winter, your dough might need a little less water, which can be a little warmer, and it can take longer to increase in size while resting and rising. So trust your instincts, and think logically: if your body is cold, you put on a sweater, have a warm drink, and try to keep your room cosy, and if you are too hot, you do the opposite—think of looking after the dough in a similar way, and the more you bake, the more you will find yourself making those kinds of small adjustments automatically.

And finally patience—the most important thing when it comes to dough! We live in a world in which we can make things happen at the touch of a button, but good breadmaking is an age-old process that requires you to slow things down, and give the dough time to develop properly. Yes, of course you can speed things up, which is exactly what big commercial bakeries have done in order to mass-produce cheap loaves with long shelf lives, but the additives that have to go into the dough, combined with the speed of production, frequently results in soft, squashy bread that many people find indigestible, so much so, that they believe that bread is bad for them (more about this on page 22). So give your dough time to rest and rise properly before baking, and your patience will be rewarded with wholesome bread with a great crumb; one that will convince you that only bad bread is bad for you!

Your three most important tools are free: your hands, your instincts, and patience.

You don't need a kitchen full of expensive gadgets to bake great bread, but you do need some essentials, (see pages 12 to 14) and the more you get hooked on breadmaking, as with any craft, you will find you collect favorite ones, old "friends" that you keep over the years. I still have the wooden rolling pin my grandfather made for me when I started out as an apprentice baker, and laying it out with the other tools that are so familiar to me, helps get me into the right, relaxed frame of mind for baking.

1 | ELECTRONIC WEIGHING SCALES

I always weigh liquids as well as flour, yeast, sugar, etc., in order to be precise, rather than reading the level in a pitcher, which is less accurate. For this reason, all liquid measures are given in grams, not milliliters.

2 | STAINLESS STEEL MIXING BOWL

You will use this all the time, not only for mixing, but for resting, and sometimes rising the dough. As a baker, I always think practically, and stainless steel is easy to handle, clean, and store. Also, since it is unbreakable, it will last forever.

3 | A STAND MIXER WITH A DOUGH HOOK

You don't *need* a mixer, but it is a great help if you are making lots of bread regularly (see page 37 for more). However, I always teach people to make dough by hand, so that they understand what it should look and feel like before they move on to a machine.

4 | EXTRA-LARGE FREEZER BAGS

As an alternative to a baking cloth, there are all kinds of special elasticated food covers available to pull over your mixing bowl in order to keep out drafts while resting the dough—people even use shower caps. However an extra-large freezer bag is all you need. I also use these to cover bowls of dough that I am resting overnight in the fridge, and to put over shaped loaves and rolls while they are rising. Avoid plastic wrap as it sticks to the dough.

5 | PLASTIC CONTAINERS

Once you start making rustic and sourdough loaves, you will need containers to store your ferments, either at ambient temperature, or in the fridge. One of the first things you learn as an apprentice baker is never to use glass. It is completely taboo, because if the glass were to break, or worse, shatter, not only would your ferment be ruined, but an entire production of dough might have to be thrown away if it was in range of any glass fragments. So if I see ferments bubbling away in attractive Mason jars, I get very nervous. Plastic is uglier, but safer!

6 | PLASTIC AND METAL SCRAPERS

My scrapers are my least expensive, yet most indispensible tools—almost extensions of my hands. I use the rounded end to mix the dough, to help turn it out from the mixing bowl in one piece ready to work it, and I use a metal scraper, or the straight edge of my plastic one for cutting, dividing, and lifting it, and keeping my work surface clean.

7 | SOFT BRUSH

A little natural fiber brush that you can keep just for breadmaking, is great for brushing excess flour and tiny scraps of dough from the work surface. In my classes, I always say to people: "the cleaner you work, the better you bake."

8 | BAKING CLOTHS

Invest in a stack of these as you will use them constantly. They are different from dishtowels, being heavier and made of a natural linen fiber. They are the traditional alternative to freezer bags to cover dough while it is resting in the mixing bowl and, unlike a cotton dishtowel, the cloth won't stick to the dough. You can also use the cloths for lining baking sheets on which to lay your shaped loaves while they rise. I just shake or brush them down well after each breadmaking session.

9 | BAKER'S COUCHE

This is a similar, but heavier, stiff natural canvas or linen cloth, which can be put on top of a baking pan and pleated to make separate "compartments" to keep a batch of loaves, such as baguettes, apart.

10 | PROVING (RISING) BASKETS

Again these are not essential, but I find that people really like them, as they are great for holding big loaves, such as sourdough, as they rise. Most are made of wicker, and lined with natural canvas or linen, but some are unlined, and leave beautiful imprinted patterns in the dough as it rises, so that the baked loaf will have a very distinctive look.

11 | PROVING (RISING) BOX

Often called a "proof box". I saw one of these and thought NO—who needs more gadgets! But then I tried one, and found it very useful in my kitchen at home, where the temperature varies far more than in the school. If you bake regularly, you will find yourself making small adjustments to the time it takes your dough to rise to just under double its size, according to how cold or warm your home is, and the box helps with this as it keeps the dough inside at a consistent temperature.

12 | LAME (DOUGH SCORING TOOL)

Essentially a lame is a razor blade fitted into a handle. It is the tool bakers use to carve their signature into a loaf. The practical purpose is to slash the top of certain loaves, such as baguettes and sourdough, in order to control the points where the expanding gas can escape, creating a "burst" in the crust as it does so (without these slashes, the crust could burst at the sides, spoiling the look of the loaf). The more aesthetic purpose is for creating distinctive patterns, crunchy edges, and different depths of golden brown in the baked bread so that bakers can personalize their loaves.

I wouldn't be without my lame, as it is designed to do the job cleanly without pulling or snagging the dough, but if you prefer, you can make the cuts with a sharp serrated knife. Scissors can also be used to snip into the tops of some breads and rolls to decorate the surface, as I have suggested in some of the recipes.

13 | PASTRY BRUSH

For brushing the tops of some breads with an egg glaze before baking.

14 | WOODEN PEEL

This is the flat wooden paddle with a long handle used by bakers and pizza chefs to slide risen loaves or pizzas smoothly and quickly into the oven (see page 99) and to pull them out again, so that the door is open for as little time as possible, to maintain the heat. There are various sizes, from small to long: about 16 x 4 inches for baguettes and about 16 x 16 inches for large loaves. You don't have to spend a lot of money on one, as the handle isn't essential; a timber yard will cut you a piece of plywood to a size

a little longer than the area you need, so you can get a grip on it. If you intend to bake several baguettes at once, it is a good idea to have about six long peels or pieces of plywood on which to load the baguettes, then slide them into the oven, one after the other.

15 | BAKING STONE OR PAN

A ceramic baking stone is the closest you can get to reproducing the hot brick floor of a baker's oven, which retains the heat, and helps to achieve an even crust on the base of the bread. You can buy specific baking stones in cooking equipment stores and some supermarkets, but for years I used pieces of granite, which did the job perfectly. Just remember, though, that while most new ovens heat up fantastically quickly and accurately, you still need to put your stone in for a good hour. You can do this at about 200°F before you turn up the temperature to the correct heat. If baking regularly, you will probably find that you leave the stone inside the oven all the time, ready to go. Alternatively, a heavy preheated baking pan turned upside down, will give you a solid flat surface.

16 | WATER SPRAY

When you combine steam with the heat of a baking stone, you get something close to the atmosphere inside a professional baker's oven, which will have automatic injections of steam. And this is what you need for certain loaves, such as baguettes and sourdough, where the crust is important. Many domestic ovens, such as those we have in the school, also have a steam option, but a simple plastic spray bottle, with which to mist the oven with water as you put in loaves, avoiding getting it on the bread itself, will do the job very well. In the recipes that follow, I suggest using one even if you have an oven with a steam system.

17 | TIMER

Never bank on remembering when to take your bread out of the oven: time it! It is so disheartening to spend hours, sometimes days, mixing, working, and resting the dough, then shaping it and rising it ready to bake, only to leave your bread in the oven until it is black, because you got distracted and forgot about it. If you have a smartphone, you can use the timer on that—so no excuses!

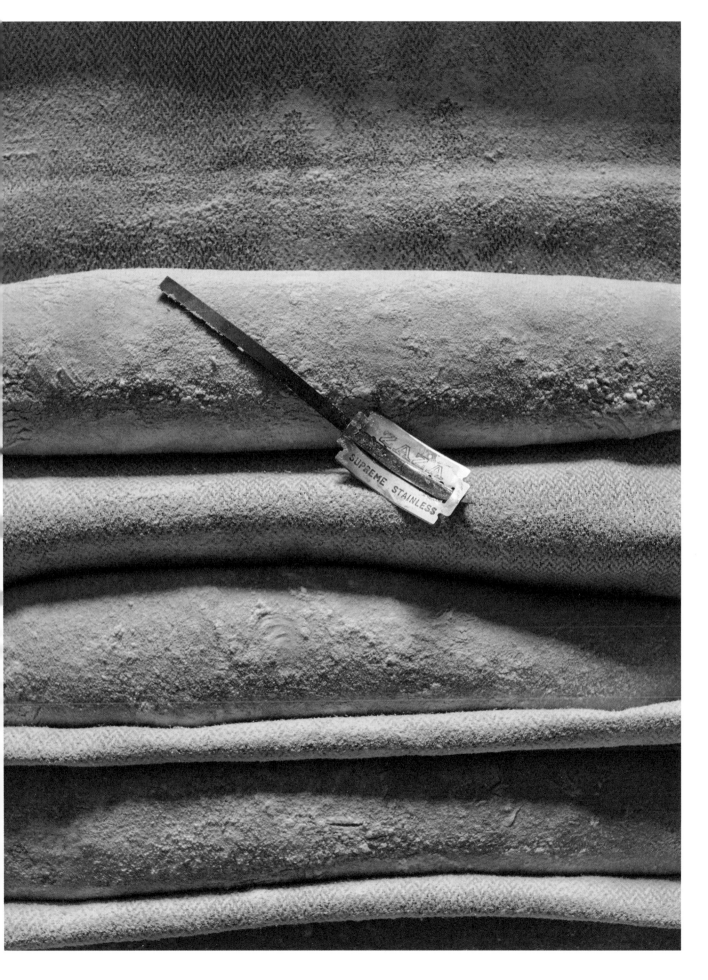

All about the crumb

When students tell me they are disappointed with the look and texture of their bread, the first thing I always want to know is how they usually make it.

If it is by hand, the answers are often more or less along these lines: "You put the ingredients in a bowl, make a well in the center, and add a little water, mix it together, and add more water if you feel it is too stiff. Flour or oil your work surface, and tip your dough out; then push down with your fist or the heel of your hand to stretch the dough. If the dough is too sticky, add more flour, and then knead vigorously until the dough is light, supple, and elastic. Then when it has risen, you need to knock it back".

I once conducted a little experiment with one of my classes, in which I gave everyone a copy of a bread recipe from a magazine, which used all the kinds of instructions above, and then left them to it. The variation in the finished results was incredible, because everyone interpreted the method differently and added varying quantities of water and extra flour, and the crumb in all the finished breads was quite heavy and dense.

My technique (and the terminology I use), is very different, but I also try to keep the recipes very specific, so that once you get the hang of working with the dough, you will find you can achieve so much more consistency in breadmaking.

Nothing about the harsh idea of kneading vigorously, or knocking back equates with the way I make my dough. I remember a potter coming along to class, and telling me that the first thing he did with his clay was to give it a good kneading to take the air out. That is the opposite of what you want to do with dough. I ask people whether they know what the dough hook on a food mixer does, and everyone understands that it is introducing air as it mixes. So why, if you are making dough by hand, would you want to do the opposite and knock out the air? It doesn't make sense to me.

Instead of kneading the dough, I prefer to talk about "working it" in a way that incorporates as much air as possible, and rather than "knocking it back," I have a more gentle way of folding it into a ball.

Nothing about the harsh idea of kneading vigorously, or knocking back equates with the way I make my dough.

It is not a technique that I invented from nowhere —it has its roots in the evolution of French baking, which I learned about as a sixteen-year-old apprentice working at my local bakery, and studying at school. There we were taught to make dough by hand in the way that it was done before mixers were invented, and so as I began my career as a baker, I realized that the old method of stretching and folding, was a brilliant one that could be adapted to the modern bakery. So, time for a quick history lesson...

In the Middle Ages, the concept of bread was that it needed to be substantial to fill you up. The flour was not of the quality we are used to today, and was most likely a blend of wheat, rye, spelt, or other grains, so the bread was heavy, dense, and hard to digest. In France, and indeed across much of Europe and elsewhere, most people made bread at home, then took it to a local bakehouse to be baked in a communal oven. Usually they would carve their initials or a design into the surface of the dough so that the baker could identify everyone's loaf. It is a practice that still happens in some countries today—I remember stumbling across a fantastic communal wood-fired oven in a bakery in Marrakesh that had been there for generations, where the local children would drop off their family's loaves, wrapped in cloth, on their way to school.

Gradually bakehouses evolved into bakeries, which were set up to make the dough, as well as to bake it, and in France, the "dough maker" was known as *le geindre* (the grunter), because his was such hard, horrible work, pummeling and pounding troughs full of stiff dough with every weapon he could think of, from his feet to his fists, batons, or big wooden paddles.

In the late 1700s, however, all that changed, when the famous French scientist, Antoine-Augustin Parmentier—the man who convinced the French that potatoes could be enjoyed by people as well as pigs— realized that by introducing more water and air into dough, it became lighter, more supple, and more responsive. And importantly, it would also grow more in volume, so once baked, the bread could feed more people, and the crumb would be much less dense and easier to digest.

This was a huge turning point for French breadmaking. From then on, bakers began to abandon the technique of bashing and kneading, in favor of a new method, using a much softer dough. Once the ingredients were mixed (*le frasage*) with a greater quantity of water—still in a big trough which could hold 220 pounds of dough—the dough was usually left for a while (an early example of the autolyze method, see page 59) then the baker would cut big lumps of it (*le découpage*), which he lifted and then threw onto the side of the trough (this was called *le passage en tête*). Next came the real revolutionary movement: the *etirage*, in which the bakers would stretch the dough from where it gripped the trough right up to their chests, and then fold it over itself, to create an air pocket. This was known as *le soufflage*: the blowing of air into the dough. The whole process would go on, probably for an hour, and since the bakers often worked bare chested, with only a cloth around them, their sweat no doubt added a certain *je ne sais quoi* to the bread! However, the result was bread that was much lighter, and far more digestible. At first, though, this didn't go down that well with the customers, who thought the bakers were charging good money for loaves full of air!

Eventually, around the 1900s, came the next revolution, when mechanical mixers began to be introduced, powered by electricity, and designed to mimic the action of the bakers' hands and introduce air in a similar way.

For me, this method of introducing air into a soft dough always made so much more sense than the idea of kneading and pummeling a stiffer dough, so I developed the technique in my own baking, and when I began teaching, I revisited and reinterpreted it in a way that would work on a smaller scale at home. The people who first came to my classes were always surprised by how much softer my dough was than they were used to, but in the last ten years, a new wave of British bakers has begun using more water, and adopting a technique similar to mine, which allows you to transform a sticky mass into a beautiful, light, airy pillow; full of life, without adding extra flour or oil.

Adopting a technique similar to mine allows you to transform a sticky mass into a beautiful, light, airy pillow.

While those early "grunting" bakers struggled with heavy, rough flour, we have come a long way since then. For our bakery and school, we work with Shipton Mill—whose founder, John Lister, has been in the milling game so long, there is no grain he doesn't know about. And with Wessex Mill, a family concern now run by fourth generation miller Paul Munsey and his daughter Emily (pictured overleaf); an amazing woman who spent five days with me at the school learning how we work with their flour. Emily is an example of the emerging band of passionate young farmers and millers, who are growing or collecting high-quality grains, and milling them slowly to avoid damaging their proteins.

Flour and water

My second question, when people tell me their bread is tight, gray, and heavy, concerns the type of flour they have been using. Often the problem is that they are using very strong bread flour, and not enough water. It is important to understand the difference between all-purpose flour, strong bread flour, and very strong bread flour. Essentially it is all about the level of the protein. All-purpose flour contains between 8 to 10 percent protein, strong bread flour 11.5 to 12.5 percent, and very strong flour can be anywhere between 13.5 to 16 percent. For breadmaking, you need a flour that is higher in protein than the all-purpose flour you would use to make cakes, because during the process of making the dough, more gluten is formed. Gluten is the protein which enables the dough to become more elastic, trapping the bubbles of gas released by the yeast as it ferments, helping the dough to rise better and give you a light, airy loaf.

All the recipes in this book use strong bread flour, and the quantity of water in the recipe is calculated for flour with this level of protein. However, one of the most common slip-ups people make, is to use a very strong flour instead, without realizing that this requires far more water to be added when mixing the dough. Without that additional water, a higher concentration of gluten forms, and the dough will feel more like a basketball than an airy pillow. And as a result, I believe the bread will be harder to digest.

In France the type of flour used for breadmaking generally contains less protein than that commonly used in the UK. Interestingly, people often tell me that when they holiday in France and buy their bread every day from the bakery, they never have that bloated feeling they often get after eating bread from the supermarket at home. Not only is there less protein in the flour, but French bakers tend to use more water. Water, like air, is a key ingredient of good bread. So when people say their dough doesn't stretch enough, I know right away that they are not adding enough water.

Very strong bread flour can be great for ciabatta, sourdoughs, etc., but just be aware that you must use

It is important to understand the difference between all-purpose flour, strong bread flour, and very strong bread flour.

more water. As a rough rule of thumb, for a plain white dough I would use 720g of water per 1kg of strong bread flour (this is more than some recipes, but will give you the nice soft dough that you need to use my technique). However if you substitute very strong flour, I would use up to 800g water.

The other issue I have with many recipes that suggest adding more flour "if necessary", is that it is all too easy to alter the make-up of the dough after you have gone to the trouble of weighing all your ingredients exactly. When people first come to classes, they don't believe that they can handle a soft, sticky dough without adding extra flour—whether it is into the dough, on their hands, or on the work surface. I have seen people use up to 300g of extra flour in this way, and when I tell students that, they are amazed. Of course the additional flour will stiffen up the dough, which causes people to panic, and fear breadmaking even more.

The combination of not using enough water, then adding more flour in order to "knead" the dough, makes it difficult to achieve the light, supple dough that is the goal. Whereas if you keep your hands out of the bag of flour, and trust in the technique, the sticky mass on your work surface will turn into a soft, shiny, and responsive dough.

Bread and health

Acres of words have been devoted to the subject of whether bread is good for you, with opinions often polarized. At one end of the scale, bread has been demonized in favor of gluten-free diets that have led to a rise in the popularity of flours made from rice, corn, potato, or legumes. At the other end, there is almost an obsession with sourdough, hailed as the pinnacle of "clean" food since it is made with natural yeasts. I don't agree with either extreme, especially the idea of one style of bread becoming elitist and expensive. Good bread is a staple that should be available to everyone. The truth is that you can have excellent bread made with fresh commercial yeast, just as you can have sourdough that is dense and indigestible made with natural yeast. It is bread that is produced on a massive industrial scale, at high speed, that has become the problem.

Some people avoid bread because they have an intolerance to wheat, or to the gluten it contains, and about one in 100 people in the US must avoid it as they suffer from celiac disease, which is an auto-immune condition caused by a reaction to gluten. However, there are many others who complain that bread makes them feel bloated and uncomfortable. Of these, I know from people who come to my classes, or have bought my books, that switching to making their own bread, or seeking out a good bakery instead of buying heavily processed, mass-produced loaves, has made a huge difference to their lives.

Good bread, made in the patient time-honored way, allows the dough to ferment slowly during the rising and proving (final rise) processes, so that the beneficial bacteria can get to work, and the finished bread is digestible. Highly processed bread, on the other hand, is made in high-speed industrial mixers that can mix 250kg of dough in 2½ minutes, so that the bakeries can churn out upwards of 10,000 loaves in a process that is all about engineers pushing buttons, not bakers using their skills. The finished bread often has such a soft, stodgy crumb, that if you scrunch a slice in your hand, it can feel almost like raw dough—no wonder it sits heavily in your stomach.

It all begins with the quality of the flour. For large-scale bakeries, grain is milled between high-speed rollers, the flour is pumped into trucks, then straight on to the bakeries, where it is sometimes used within 18 hours of it being processed. At this point the fresh flour is quite unstable so, in order to make it behave on a huge scale, dough "conditioners" or "improvers," emulsifiers, and sometimes high levels of fast-action yeast or extra gluten, have to be added.

By contrast, the flour we use in our bakery is milled more slowly, then aged for a certain time before we receive it. This helps to stabilize it, so that it behaves in the same way as the flour you buy to make bread at home, which will have rested naturally as it sits on the store shelf. I liken the process to the hanging of meat, which allows it to cure a little, and become more digestible. The practice of resting flour, (known in France as *avoir du plancher*), was traditionally done in Britain and across Europe. From reading old books, I can see that bakers never dreamed of using fresh flour. But that has been lost in the demand for fast, cheap bread. Just as well-hung meat is more expensive due to the cost of special aging rooms, the price of a standard loaf would increase if the big bakeries had to maintain storage space for resting flour.

One of my biggest bugbears is the use of "clean declaration improvers" in the industrial baking process, which allows the addition of amylase and other enzymes, without these being shown on the label since they are classified as "processing aids." They are cheating devices, which I hope and believe will soon be outlawed.

The assumption is that whole-wheat bread is superior, as using flour milled from whole grains means that the nutrients are not stripped out. But if it is made using the same fast industrial process, it is not necessarily much better for you. In fact, since whole-wheat flour is heavier, it can be even more indigestible. The same misconception can also apply to breads labeled "artisan" or "rustic," words that are frequently abused, as they have no official definition, but have become a marketing ploy, which can allow bread to be presented as something special, while still being made with the same "clean declaration improvers."

Bake and repeat

Sometimes people who have attended my five-day breadmaking course ask: "Which class should I do next?" If they have been baking bread for the first time, my answer is usually: "Come back and do it again." Why? Of course I can teach new recipes, but that isn't what you need when you first start to make bread: instead it is experience, and that comes through repetition. The more you repeat, the more you understand, begin to focus on particular aspects of the whole process, and gain confidence and consistency in your results. Becoming good at baking is like golf or fly-fishing. It is not enough to have a few lessons, and away you go; the skill comes with practice, and the experience of different situations.

The key is to get into a routine and rhythm of baking regularly. If you just make the odd loaf once a month, it is hard to get the momentum going. Undoubtedly your friends will say you have turned into a baking bore, but they will love the bread you give them!

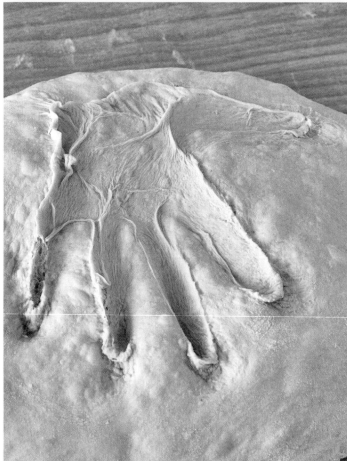

Rest and rise

I find there is quite a lot of confusion around the terminology of the various stages at which the dough is left to rise. I like to keep it simple, so I only use two terms: resting and rising.

Once the dough has been worked into a smooth dough by hand or machine, it needs to be formed into a ball in order to rest for the time suggested in each recipe. Then, after it has been rested and either put into pans, or divided and shaped into loaves, rolls, or baguettes it needs to be left to rise. Both resting and rising allow the d ough to develop and mature.

As all the books will tell you, the dough should be covered (either with a baking cloth, or for preference, a large freezer bag that also keeps out any drafts, see page 12). For the best results, the dough should be rested or risen in a warm, draft-free place, about 75 to 77°F. If the room is a little chilly, it will be slower to respond, or if it is too warm, the dough will move more quickly.

The questions I am always asked are: "How long can I rest/rise the dough for?"; "How will I know when it is ready?" and "What happens if I leave it too long, or not long enough?"

The answer, when resting or rising dough, is that, although I have given guidelines, you decide how long to leave it: take control. You can rest or rise dough at room temperature for the time suggested in the recipe, or you can leave it longer—even overnight, if you wish, if you put it in the fridge (covered with a freezer bag to prevent a skin forming on the top of the dough). Using the fridge slows things down (especially useful if your kitchen is very warm) so the dough is ready when you want it to be. For example, if you want to bake fresh bread for dinner, you can make your dough in the morning, shape it and leave it rising in the fridge ready to finish off and bake later, with the added bonus that the longer you leave it, the more the flavor, structure, and therefore the crumb, will develop.

You can tell if the dough has over-rested, because, instead of being strong, bouncy, and beautifully domed, it will appear a little weak and deflated.

The answer, when resting or rising your dough, is that you decide how long to leave it for: take control.

Think of a balloon after a few days: it starts to sag and wrinkle, and look a bit sad.

The reason I suggest leaving the dough to rest until "just under" rather than double in size, which is the usual instruction, is that I find it helps people to pay attention and guard against reaching this deflating stage. However, if it does happen, don't worry, you can still rescue it by taking it out of the bowl, re-forming it into a ball, then returning it to the bowl (see pages 50 to 52) to begin the resting process again.

Over-rising is a different matter, and one of the things that I find people worry about most. It is better to bake dough when it is slightly under-risen, than to try to do anything with over-risen dough. You will know immediately if your dough is over-risen, because as soon as you turn it out of its proving basket, lift it onto a peel, or cut into the top of it with a lame, it will deflate. Don't be tempted to try and bake it because the bad news is that there is no oven fairy to wave a wand; you will end up with something with a very dense and unappetizing crumb. Nor can you achieve a good crumb by re-folding the dough at this stage, and starting again. All isn't quite lost, though, because you could use the raw dough as a ferment to add to, and enhance, your next batch of dough (see page 94 for how to refresh the ferment and keep it going).

Mist and heat

In an ordinary domestic oven, creating steam by misting the dough, works in conjunction with slashing the tops of certain breads, such as baguettes and sourdoughs. (You don't need steam for enriched doughs, which are glazed with egg because, as well as giving the surface a pleasing shine, the glaze keeps the bread moist too.) The steam softens the texture of the top of baguettes and rustic breads, keeping it moist, and prevents a crust from forming too quickly. If you don't introduce steam, the crust could burst too soon and in the wrong places, as the gas expands in the oven. By delaying the formation of the crust, you allow the crumb to develop evenly before the crust forms, and bursts through the slashes you have made in the top of the loaf. Without steam, not only do you risk your loaf bursting out on the sides, but the crumb can look dull, tight and unappetizing.

Ideally use a baking stone (see page 14), which will need a good hour to heat through thoroughly before you bake your loaf on top, even if your oven heats up from cold to 400°F in seven minutes.

When baking breads that have a distinct crust (baguettes or sourdoughs, for example), very slightly open the oven door for the last 4 to 5 minutes of baking time. Professional bakers' ovens have a "damper," a trap at the back of the oven, that allows the steam to escape, so that the bread finishes baking in dry heat, to thicken and crisp the crust so that it holds, and doesn't soften when the bread comes out of the oven. By leaving the door slightly ajar, you can achieve the same thing using a domestic oven.

Timing

One thing I find is that most people under-bake bread. Being French, I am used to much more caramelization in baking, so I like a bread to be quite dark golden, but I think people are often scared of burning it. I always say, not least because everyone's oven is a little different: don't just put your bread in the oven and blindly set the timer for the baking time given in the recipe. Set it for 3 minutes. Look and check. And then set it for an additional 3 minutes. That way you stay switched on and start judging the baking time for yourself.

The age-old practice of tapping the base of a loaf to see if it sounds hollow (therefore ready to come out of the oven), is a good one, but I think it should also be combined with an emphasis on color (and steam where this is relevant). For example, a baguette that is light golden and sounds hollow on the base may seem perfect, but, after a little cooling, the crust can soften, whereas some steam and a little more time to darken in the oven, can make all the difference.

Being French, I am used to much more caramelization in baking, so I like a bread to be quite dark golden, but I think people are often scared of burning it.

Show the dough who's boss

Hands
Machine
Dough

I learned way back as an apprentice, that before you start using a machine to make dough, you need to learn how to make it by hand, so that you really feel the dough, get to understand it, and learn to be in control of it. *Le Patron* who taught us put it this way: "Machines were made to mimic hands, but if you don't know what your hands are supposed to do, how can you tell the mixer what to do?" I have been amazed and humbled that so many professional bakers—even French bakers—have come to my classes in recent years, because they are aware that they have lost touch with feeling the dough responding in their hands, since they use big mechanical mixers all the time, and they have left feeling re-energized about the whole baking process. "Show the dough who's boss" has become the mantra in my baking classes. This is the phrase that has stuck in my head since I first went into the mixing room at my local bakery and was given a massive lump of soft, sticky dough to work with. It stuck to my hands and to the table and I started to panic. That was when *Le Patron* told me, "*Il faut maîtriser la pâte!*" which roughly translates as "You have to show the dough who's boss." "If you fear it," he continued, "it *will* stick. Until you take control, you won't be able to move on." I learned very quickly that I couldn't blame the dough; it was me making the dough sticky, because I didn't understand what I was doing.

"Show the dough who's boss" has become the mantra in my baking classes. This is the phrase that has stuck in my head since I first went into the mixing room at my local bakery and was given a massive lump of soft, sticky dough to work with.

Many people who join my five-day classes find that, on the first day when they start making dough, they have that same fear. They don't believe that they will be able to handle the stickiness of the dough without using additional flour but, once they allow themselves to trust in the technique set out on the pages that follow, by the end of the class on Friday, they are buzzing, and extremely proud of themselves.

If you are new to breadmaking, or looking to make bread in a different way, I urge you to begin by making bread by hand until you build up confidence in your relationship with the dough. I suggest you work using 1kg of flour because the dough responds better with more volume. You can always give away any loaves you can't use immediately—it is good to get feedback from friends and family—or you can freeze them.

Hands

The recipe that I always start off with in my classes is for white baguettes. I call it my foundation dough, because it can also be used for simple pan loaves, or rolls as well (see page 38), and I think it teaches all the basic techniques: mixing and working the dough, dividing, shaping, rising, carving your signature cuts in the top, and finally baking with steam to give a light, airy crumb and a characteristic crunchy "burst" in the crust.

I tell people to forget the terminology and just think of "wet water", which everyone finds very funny.

In classes, after I have demonstrated making dough by hand without kneading, before people try this for themselves, I ask them to work in small groups and share out loud the steps involved. This allows them to visualize the whole process before they start, otherwise I find the instinct is to switch off, and turn to the recipe. I want everyone to think a few steps ahead, otherwise it is easy to lose focus, and become indecisive about what happens next. Remember, you need to show the dough who's boss!

A note about the temperature of water: experience tells me that there are too many attempts at describing the ideal temperature of water when you are mixing dough by hand: body temperature, blood temperature, room temperature, warm, lukewarm—even "just right," whatever that means. So, in my classes I ask everyone to close their eyes, then I put out three glasses of water per table: one is hot, another is cold, and, in the middle, one that I have mixed to the right temperature. Then I ask people to put their fingers into the glass of hot water and tell me what they feel, then put their fingers into the

cold water and again say what they feel. No one has any difficulty in identifying hot and cold, but all sorts of expressions are used to describe the water in the middle glass, because it doesn't trigger any particular sensations.

I tell people to forget the terminology and just think of "wet water," which everyone finds very funny. But what I actually mean is that it is completely neutral. You feel nothing in particular when you put your fingers into it. This is the temperature you need your water to be when you mix dough by hand. In the recipes in this book, if the ingredients simply state "water," you know that I mean neither warm nor cool. Once you start using a mixer, it is different, and you should always use cool water; but more about this on page 37.

Another reminder, this time about the flour, and I can't say this often enough: once you have mixed all the ingredients in your bowl, don't put any flour (or oil) on the work surface before you turn the dough out onto it. I know all your instincts will be to do this. You will look at this sticky oatmeal-like mass, and think you can't handle it without at least flouring your hands, but trust me: you don't need it, and your dough will be better off without it.

Even when you have worked the dough, and you are ready to form it into a ball to leave it to rest (step 18 on page 49), only very lightly dust the work surface with flour—by that I mean just skim it over the top—so that it doesn't spoil the smooth surface of the dough.

Machine

Once you are confident about making the dough by hand, you might want to try using a mixer with a dough hook, as it can make life easier. One of the questions I am asked most, is: "How do you know when the dough is ready?" Sometimes people tell me that they start off using a mixer, and then finish it off by hand, as they are unsure whether they have done enough in the mixer. That is why you need to bring your experience of using your hands to the process of using a machine, so you can recognize when it has reached the same stage of feeling bouncy and alive.

First ensure that the water is cool (rather than "wet water" (see page 35), which is what you need for mixing by hand). This is because the mechanical action of the mixer generates heat in the dough (which doesn't happen when you work it by hand), so if you start off with warmer liquid, the dough could overheat, causing it to lose its strength and become impossible to use.

The only thing a mixer cannot do is form the important top and bottom of the dough, and then fold it into a ball ready to rest.

For simple doughs made with flour, yeast, salt, and water, just pour in the water first (remember it should be cool), add the flour and salt, and break up the yeast roughly on top keeping it separate from the salt (see page 38). (Note that for enriched doughs, when you are using additional ingredients, such as milk, eggs, and butter, these should be added in a specific order as stated in each recipe).

Mix for 4 minutes on slow speed. This stage is comparable to mixing all your ingredients (steps 1 to 7 on pages 38 to 40). The next stage is the equivalent of steps 8 to 17 in the process by hand on pages 41

to 49. Turn the mixer speed up to medium (usually setting 3 or 4, depending on the model), and observe what is happening.

For the first 6 to 7 minutes, the base of the bowl will feel cold, but after about 10 to 12 minutes, you will see the dough start to come away from the sides of the bowl. At this stage, the bowl will start to warm up, and the mixer will usually move a little as the dough is starting to become stronger, and the motor is having to work harder. Every dough is slightly different, and some may take about 15 minutes to reach this stage.

From this point it will take about an additional 3 to 5 minutes, again depending on the particular dough, until it comes away completely cleanly from the sides: you will hear it make a flapping sound as it does so.

The important thing when mixing dough with a machine, is not to become impatient and turn the mixer up to a fast speed. If you do that, the temperature will rise too quickly, and you will ruin the dough. So don't rush it.

The only thing a mixer cannot do is form the important top and bottom of the dough, and then fold it into a ball ready to rest. So now you need to use your scraper to transfer the dough to a very lightly floured work surface, and follow steps 19 to 23 on pages 49 to 52.

Whether you have made the dough by hand, or in a mixer, in the next chapter, I will show you how to use it to make baguettes (see page 61).

Dough

**THIS IS MY FOUNDATION
DOUGH WHICH MAKES
ENOUGH DOUGH FOR
8 SMALL BAGUETTES**

1kg strong white bread flour
20g fine sea salt
20g compressed fresh yeast
720g water

1 Put the flour in a large bowl, break up the yeast on one side of the bowl and place the salt on the other side. It is important to keep them apart as they are both powerful and if mixed together, the salt will suck all the moisture from the yeast and they will both "die".

2 Lightly rub the yeast into the flour using the flats of your hands—as if you were washing them.

3 Now you can mix the flour, yeast, and salt together.

4 Pour in all the water in one go—don't be scared!

5 Use the rounded end of your scraper to mix everything together, working around and around in one direction, and turning the bowl in the opposite direction as you go.

6 Make sure that you use the scraper to pick up all the flour from the bottom of the bowl as you mix.

7 The dough will feel very sticky at first, but trust in the technique, take your time, and keep mixing until there are no dry bits, and the sides of the bowl become clean all the way around with no flour showing. The temptation is to rush this stage, but the more work you do in the bowl, the better.

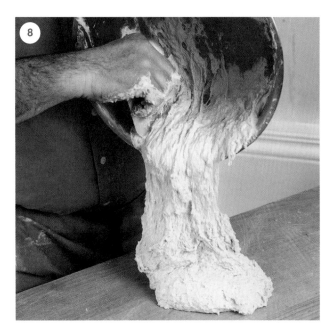

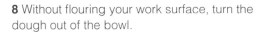

8 Without flouring your work surface, turn the dough out of the bowl.

Use a scraper to ensure the bowl is perfectly clean, because you are going to put the dough back into the bowl to rest once you have worked it, and you don't want any dry scraps of dough to stick to it. The dough should appear like a sticky porridge, with no patches of flour and no water showing.

9 Now the task is to transform that sticky mass into a tidy shape that you can work with. You will see this step more clearly on my videos online, but to do this, you need to keep your scraper almost flat against your work surface, and use it to skim the dough so that it spins around.

In my classes I call this technique taking the dough for a walk, because it really helps if you walk up and down as you do this. Avoid the natural reflex to flip the dough over, because you will quickly see that the dough forms a distinct top and bottom. The bottom will stay sticky (as in the picture above). Now you are ready to start working the dough. The first thing to perfect is the way you stand behind the work surface. Don't lean against it, but stand a little way back, and put one foot forward. Don't have your hands rigidly in front of you, but bend your elbows out to the sides (imagine you are a gorilla!).

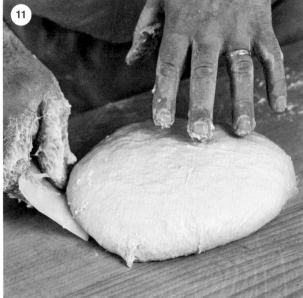

10 The top will have a natural smooth skin forming over it, and by ensuring the top is always on top, and the bottom on the bottom, you are in control. It is a small detail, but a huge step in understanding the way that dough behaves.

11 Repeat this skimming movement a few times until the top is smooth, though the bottom will still be sticky. Remember the skimming technique, because you will come back to this step several times.

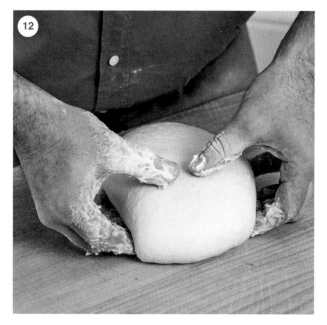

12 Shift your weight onto your front foot and at the same time slide your fingers underneath the dough as if they were forks, and scoop it up so that it "pops" cleanly off the work surface and doesn't drag. When you do this your whole body gets behind the movement, not just your arms. The power is coming from your legs and your core, so you can work with big quantities of dough without struggling. Don't be tempted to grip the dough tightly: the lighter the touch, the better.

In one movement, as you lift up the dough, turn your hands toward you, so that the dough swings.

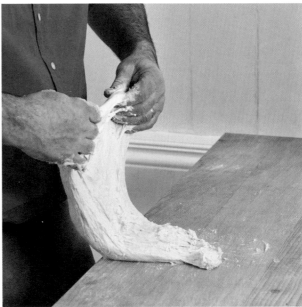

13 Slap it down "tail first" on the work surface. By slap, I refer to the sound of the tail of the dough as it comes into contact with the work surface. It isn't meant to be a hard, aggressive movement. You just want the dough to cling to the surface a little, which will allow you to stretch it.

14 Stretch the dough upwards and outwards, and then forward over itself like a wave. By doing this you form a big air pocket.

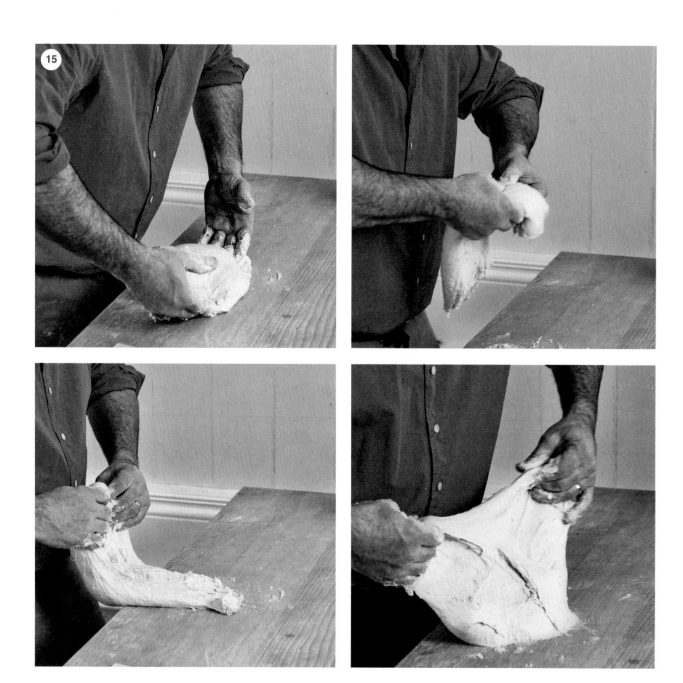

15 Slide your fingers underneath again, and get into a rhythm of repeating the sequence 4 or 5 times, then skimming (step 9), repeating and skimming...

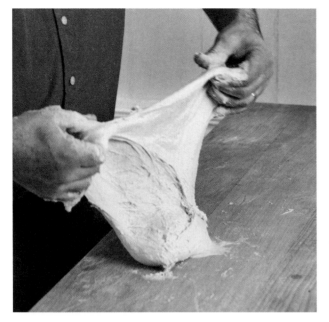

Keep repeating until the dough becomes stronger and more elastic, and alive. The important thing is to relax, and get into a rhythm of rocking onto your front foot as you scoop up the dough and let it swing, then rocking backwards as you slap it down, and forwards again as you stretch it over itself.

Once you get used to this cycle of a few slaps, then skimming, a few more slaps, then skimming, you will be surprised how quickly the dough loses its stickiness and comes away from your hands, and eventually becomes smooth and a little wobbly to the touch. With a bit of practice, the skimming and slapping process should take no more than 10 minutes.

16 After the final skim, the dough should feel tighter and stronger, and the film on the surface of the dough should be stretching all the way around and underneath the dough, so that it no longer feels sticky to the touch.

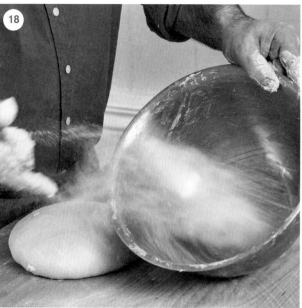

17 To finish off, repeat the slapping movement, but this time, have your hands in the starting position shown in the picture above. Repeat the movement three or four times, giving the dough a quarter turn between each one.

18 Very lightly skim your work surface and bowl with flour.

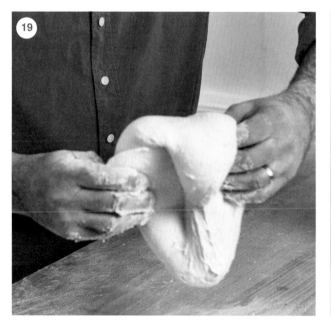

19 Turn the dough over so that it is now bottom-side up.

20 Now you need to form the dough into a ball. Gather each "corner" of the dough and fold into the center, pressing down lightly with your thumb. Use your other hand to rotate the dough counter-clockwise before folding in the next "corner." Repeat the folding and rotating sequence an additional six times to strengthen the dough.

21 Finally turn the dough over so your top is back on top, and smooth and shape it into a round.

22 Use a scraper to help you lift the dough into your floured bowl.

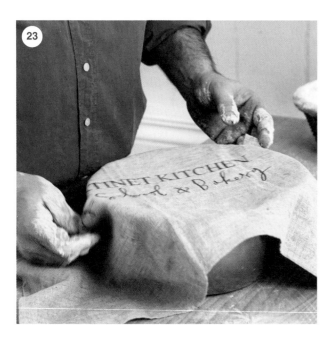

23 Cover with a baking cloth or a large freezer bag and leave the dough to rest for the time suggested in the recipe until just under double in size. I always advise "just under" double to give you a little leeway, so you are unlikely to over-rest it (see page 27).

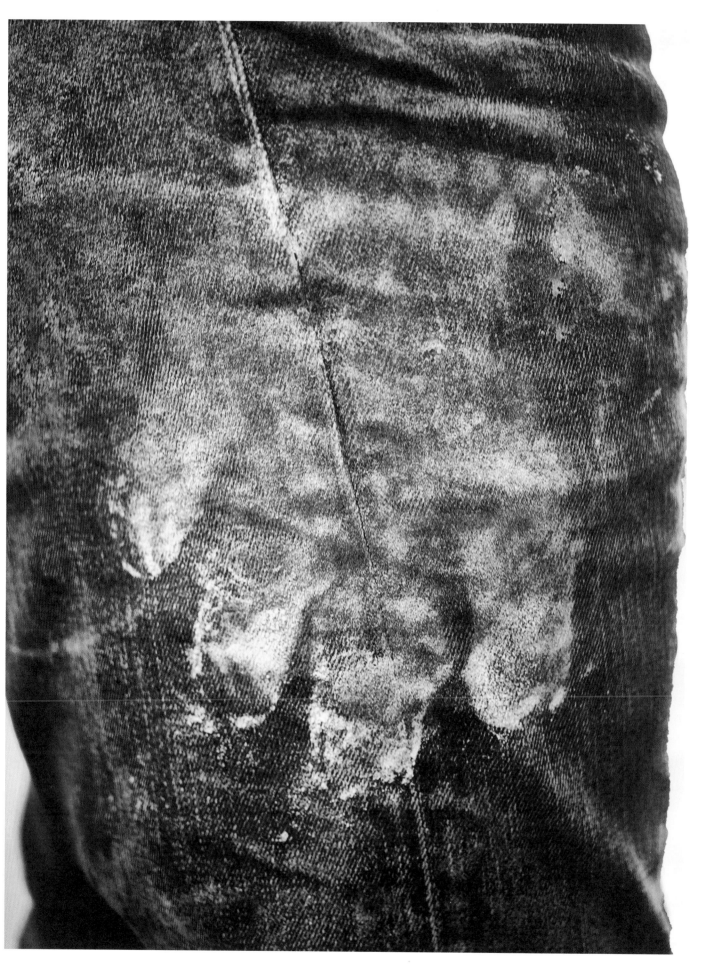

Rustic and sourdough

In my five-day breadmaking class, I don't even mention sourdough until day three or four, because the very idea of sourdough seems to have taken on almost mythical proportions. People often tell me that they have been given a sourdough "starter" by a friend, but they don't know what to do with it and have "killed" it, so they feel guilty. And there is so much misunderstanding of what sourdough actually is. There is a notion that it is a particular bread, whereas the word just describes the process of making bread by harnessing the natural fermentation of wild yeasts in everyday ingredients like yogurt, honey, or fruit, rather than compressed fresh commercial yeast. Most countries and communities have developed their own terms for these natural cultures, on which you build your bread; terms like *biga*, *poolish*, starter, or sponge all refer to the same concept.

The history of sourdough goes back to ancient times. As far back as the neolithic age, there is evidence of grain being ground, probably to make flatbread, and it was always going to be a matter of time before someone would leave a mixture of water and wheat flour to ferment, probably by accident, but bake it anyway, only to discover that the natural wild yeasts that had formed, caused the dough to rise. Fermented breads crop up in cultures all over the world from Ethiopia to the Sudan, but the first recorded leavened (risen) breads, are usually attributed to the Ancient Egyptians, whose wall paintings show they knew how to harness natural yeasts in both beer and breadmaking. However up until the nineteenth century, when compressed fresh commercial yeasts were developed, any risen dough, wherever it was produced, was sourdough.

One reason sourdough is so valued—apart from its flavor—is that the process of slow fermentation over several days makes the finished bread very digestible, which explains why so many people find they can enjoy sourdough, without experiencing the discomfort and bloating that can be caused by eating the type of bread produced cheaply and quickly by industrial processes.

Whereas previous generations became well versed in the art of fermentation, understanding how to use the natural yeasts that are all around us, not only to make bread at home, but also wine, beer, cheese, and charcuterie, in our modern age, we have become more detached from such skills, and it takes a bit of time and patience to understand and master them again. So rather than jumping straight to sourdough, I recommend you work up to it step by step, and first build confidence perfecting the techniques involved in working, resting, rising and baking a simple dough, as described in the previous chapter, until you feel comfortable with baking. Next, you can slow down the resting and maturing of this dough by putting it in the fridge for several hours or overnight—just by doing this, as you can see from page 27, you add real depth of flavor and character to the crumb and crust. From here you can progress to making bread with simple ferments, but still

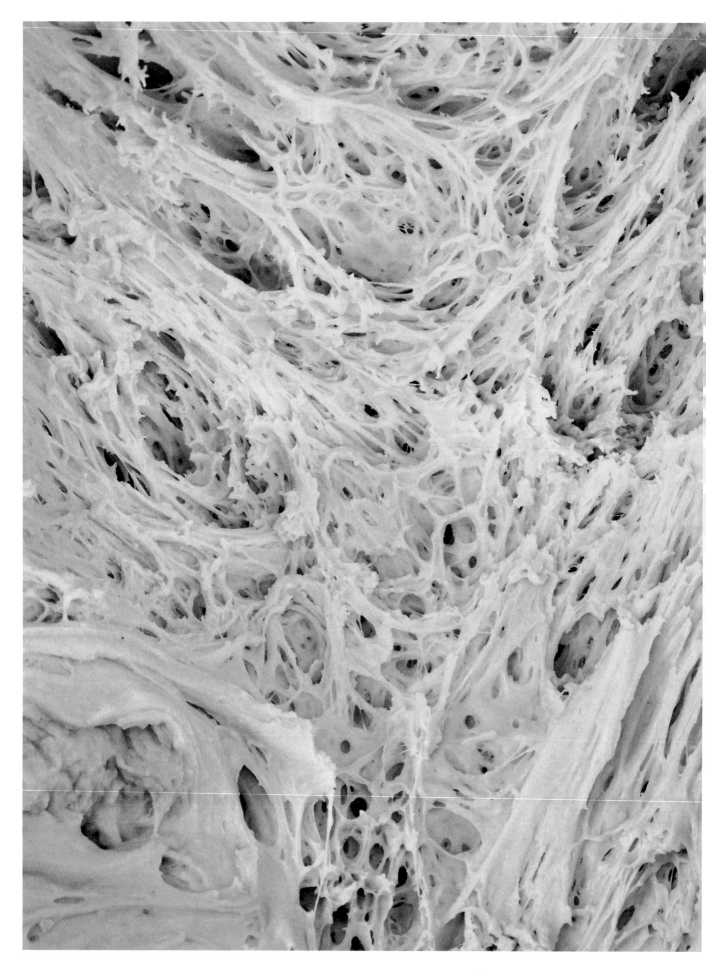

use some compressed fresh commercial yeast in your recipe. By starting with even the most basic ferment made with strong flour, water, and yeast, you will enhance the depth of flavor and texture of the crumb and crust and you can also use ale or cider instead of water, and experiment with some different flours. Such is the mystique of sourdough that people can be very dismissive of using any kind of compressed fresh commercial yeast in a ferment, but bakers have been making excellent bread in this way for centuries.

If you bake simple white bread (using the foundation dough on page 38) every few days, one way to gradually reduce the quantity of compressed fresh commercial yeast in your dough and edge toward bread leavened by natural yeasts, is to keep back 400g of dough when you reach the dividing stage, ready to rise it. Place the portion of dough in a bowl, covered, in your fridge for up to 48 hours (no more, or it will lose its strength). This becomes your ferment, and you can use it to make your next batch of dough. To do this, put the fermented dough straight from the fridge into the bowl of your mixer, add 1kg strong flour, 20g salt and 720g water as usual, but omit the yeast, then carry on mixing your dough in the normal way. Your fermented dough will become absorbed as you mix. Then, when you reach the resting stage, keep back 400g of this dough, as before. You can keep repeating this process until the original compressed fresh commercial yeast has become so diluted, that you end up with something close to sourdough, though it can't be labeled as such, because pure sourdough must be made using a natural culture. Your bread will take longer to rest and rise as the yeast becomes more natural, so this is a good way of mastering a slower way of baking, before progressing to sourdough proper.

This technique can also be used if you happen to over-prove your dough (see page 27). Just refold it into a ball, following steps 20 to 23 on pages 50 to 52 and keep 400g of it to use as a ferment as above.

In this chapter I have also included recipes that build on what bakers call a "soaker": a mixture of flour or grains and water, left for at least 15 to 20 minutes (or longer, even overnight). This is not a ferment, but another, centuries-old, way of making bread. The soaker introduces additional water into the dough, which helps to release the starch in the flour, adding extra life and softness to the crumb, so the bread will keep a little longer. Originally it would have been used if the flour for breadmaking was a little weak. It is a variation on the idea of resting the mixture of flour and water before stretching and folding it, that was introduced by French bakers in the second half of the eighteenth century (see page 18). This was later reinvented in commercial breadmaking in 1974 as the "autolyze method" by Professor Raymond Calvel, a research chemist, who discovered as far back as the 1960s that the simple resting of the flour and water before adding salt and yeast, resulted in bread with "a creamy crumb, excellent flavor, and a very good quality overall." It is an idea that has been reinvented yet again more recently in the fashion for no-knead bread, which relies on the long resting of the dough, which is not worked or shaped, but baked in a pot.

> By starting with even the most basic ferment made with strong flour, water, and yeast, you will enhance the depth of flavor and texture of the crumb and crust.

Rustic baguettes

By adding a simple flour, water, and yeast ferment to the basic white baguette recipe, you can achieve a more waxy, open crumb, and a great flavor that is a little more acidic. If you wish, enhance the flavor further by using beer or cider instead of water, or vary the flour. I have added some rye flour to the recipe, but you can use all white flour if you prefer. Once the dough is made, it is rested in the fridge for at least a couple of hours, but for the best results, leave it for 24 hours. All of these elements help to develop the structure of the bread, and add to the depth of flavor.

You can make your dough by hand following the steps on pages 38 to 52, but I have given the method using a mixer. You can divide the baguette dough in two, but it is more responsive in greater volume.

MAKES 8 SMALL BAGUETTES

470g water
700g strong white bread flour, plus extra for dusting
50g rye flour
20g fine sea salt
10g compressed fresh yeast
semolina flour, for dusting the peels and pans

For the ferment:
250g strong bread flour
5g compressed fresh yeast
250g cool water

1 Start by making the ferment: put the flour in a mixing bowl, break up the yeast, and lightly rub it into the flour using the flats of your hands.

2 Pour in all the water, and mix to an oatmeal consistency. Cover with a clean baking cloth or a freezer bag, large enough to cover the bowl, and leave to rest for 3 hours (see page 27).

3 To make the dough, transfer the ferment to a food mixer, add the water, then the flours and salt, and roughly break up the yeast on top on the opposite side of the bowl to the salt. Mix for 4 minutes on slow speed, then turn up to medium for about an additional 12 minutes, until you have a dough that comes away cleanly from the edges of the bowl.

4 Turn out the dough using your scraper onto a lightly floured work surface, and also lightly flour a clean bowl.

5 Form the dough into a ball following steps 20 to 23 on pages 50 to 52, place the dough in the bowl, cover, and leave to rest for about 45 minutes until just under double in size (see page 27).

6 Turn out the dough, re-form into a ball as above, and leave to rest for an additional 30 minutes, as before.

7 Now put the bowl in the fridge for a couple of hours at least, up to 24 hours, depending on when you want to bake your baguettes (see page 68).

8 When you are ready to bake, take the bowl of dough from the fridge. Touch the top with the back of your hand, and if the dough feels quite wet and sticky, dust it with a little flour.

9 Lightly flour the work surface, and use your scraper to run around the edge of the dough to help release it from the bowl.

10 Tip the dough onto the work surface so the top is now underneath, using your scraper to ensure the bowl is completely clean.

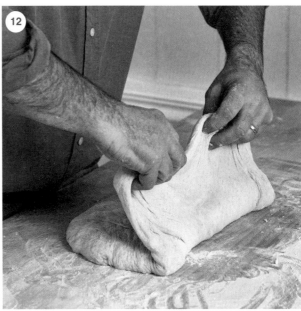

11 Dust the surface of the dough very lightly with flour, and with the flats of your hands, quickly and gently tap it into a rough square.

12 Fold the top half of the dough into the center.

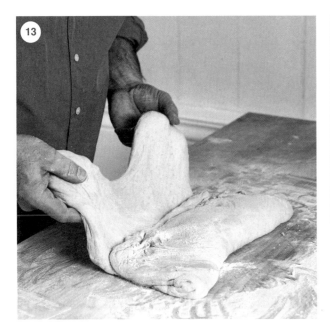

13 Fold the other half of the dough over the top to create the layers.

14 Finally fold the dough along its length, and turn it over, so that the seam is underneath.

15 Use the round end of your scraper to divide the dough into 8 equal square-shaped pieces. Each should weigh about 220g. (By weighing each piece you will help them to bake consistently).

16 Dust a large baker's couche (see page 12) or a thick baking cloth with flour.

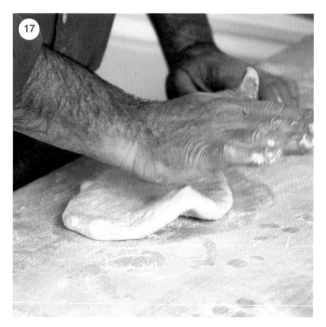

17 Turn over each piece of dough so that the top is now underneath, and with the heel of your hand, flatten it into a rough rectangle.

18 Fold the top half of the dough toward you into the center (always fold the dough toward you, to give you more control).

19 Press it down, again with the heel of your hand.

20 Turn the dough through 360 degrees, so that the fold is facing you.

21 Fold the top half of the dough toward you into the center, and press it down as before. This will form the "spine" of the baguette.

22 Now you need to fold the dough again lengthwise to seal the edges. Starting at the right-hand side (if you are right-handed), work your way along as quickly as you can, using the forefinger and thumb of your left hand to twist the dough slightly toward you.

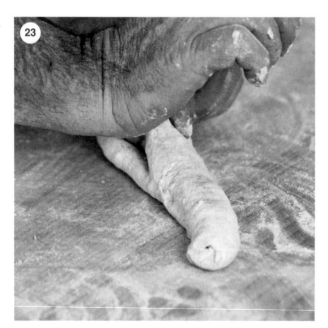

23 Press down along the length with the heel of your right hand so the spine is underneath.

24 Roll each end firmly backwards and forwards between your fingers so that the ends become pointed. Do the same with the seven remaining pieces.

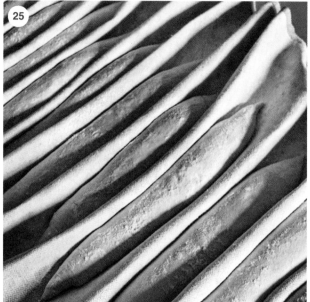

25 Lay each baguette, seam-side down, on the floured couche or baking cloth, making a pleat in between, to keep them separate. Leave to rise for 45 minutes to 1 hour, until just under double in size. If you press the tops lightly, the dough should bounce back.

26 Preheat the oven to 475°F and put in two baking stones or sheets. Remember that baking stones will need a good hour to heat through. Dust your loading peels or baking trays with semolina – the grains act like rollers so your bread will slide over them easily into the oven.

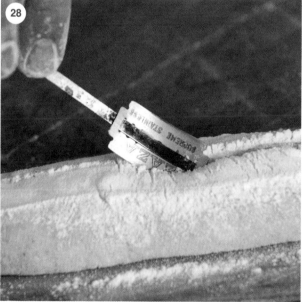

27 Use another wooden peel to transfer each baguette to the "loading" peels or baking pans.

28 Dust the top of each baguette with flour, and with your lame (see page 28) at a 45 degree angle, make either a single long cut along the top of the baguette, or two or three diagonal ones, making the cuts as quickly and cleanly as you can to avoid dragging the dough.

29 Fill a clean spray bottle with water.

30 Slide the baguettes from the peels or baking pans onto the preheated stones or pans in the oven. Quickly mist the oven generously with your water spray, pumping it for about 5 to 6 seconds, and avoiding spraying the baguettes as much as possible.

31 Bake for 18 to 20 minutes, opening the oven so that it is very slightly ajar for the last 3 to 4 minutes to allow some steam to escape. This will help to create a good crust. The baguettes should be deep golden on top, and a lighter golden underneath, and the base should feel firm. You should be able to hear the crust "sing" as the hot crust cracks in the cooler air outside the oven.

What a difference a day (or night) makes

The crust and crumb of your bread will change quite dramatically in texture and flavor simply by resting the dough for several hours, preferably overnight, in the fridge, covered with a large freezer bag, big enough to cover the entire bowl. When you are ready to make your bread, use the dough straight from the fridge.

Bakers call this technique "retarding rising." Slowing the process by refrigerating the dough will give your bread a far more open texture, a sharp crisp crust with a more pronounced burst, and a flavor that is a little more acidic, yet sweeter at the same time. You can see the difference in the appearance of the crumb in the photograph: the dough for the baguette on the left was rested for about 3 hours (out of the fridge), whereas the dough for the baguette on the right was rested in the fridge overnight.

The final cut

In France a traditional baguette will be slashed along the top with a lame; however, there is nothing to stop you from decorating any bread you make in your own way. When I look on social media, I am so impressed at the incredible artistry people are bringing to their baking: carving designs and using stencils to etch patterns into the crusts of their loaves to make them really stand out.

As well as a lame or a small serrated-edged knife, scissors are a great tool for creating interesting effects in the crust, for example, cuts simply made in a diamond shape give a hedgehog effect when the baguette is baked. The key is to make quick, decisive snips in the dough as, just as when using a lame, you want to avoid dragging and snagging.

Often in French bakeries, you will see *pain épi* alongside the boxes of baguettes slashed in the top. *Epi* means an "ear of wheat" and the idea is that everyone can pull off their own 'ear' from the loaf.

The *epi* is made in the same way as the baguette, but instead of slashing the top, the ears are formed with scissor cuts. You need to hold these at a 45° angle to the dough, then, beginning at one end, open the scissors out to the width of the baguette, and snip quickly, cutting three quarters of the way through the dough. This creates a "V" shaped point of dough, which you can push out to one side. Make a similar cut a little further along the length of the top, and then push the pointed dough to the opposite side. Continue in the same way along the length of the bread, so the finished effect is of a head of wheat. Now you can bake it, using steam, in the same way as a baguette, until the crust is golden, crunchy, and delicious.

As well as a lame or a small serrated-edged knife, scissors are a great tool for creating interesting effects in the crust.

Fougasse with Gruyère, bacon, and caramelized garlic

The cover of my first book, *Dough*, featured a leaf-shaped fougasse. It is still a huge favorite, as it is quick and simple to achieve something that looks fantastic, and so it gives everyone a boost of confidence. However, for this book, I wanted to include a slightly more advanced version with a different character, so this recipe uses an ale ferment, and the dough is stuffed with garlic, bacon cubes, and Gruyère cheese before baking (if you like, you can sprinkle on a little more before the bread goes into the oven).

Enjoy these breads freshly baked in the evening, or you can part-bake them in a preheated oven at 450°F for 7 to 8 minutes earlier in the day, let them cool, then wrap them in waxed paper until you are ready to finish the baking process at the same temperature for an additional 7 to 8 minutes. Or you can wrap the part-baked breads in waxed paper, put them in freezer bags, tie them tightly and freeze ready for another time. Defrost the fougasses for 30 minutes, then finish baking them at 450°F for an additional 8 to 9 minutes.

---

1 Start by making the ferment. Put the rye flour in a mixing bowl, break up the yeast, and lightly rub it into the flour using the flats of your hands.

2 Mix in the ale, then cover the bowl with a clean baking cloth or a large freezer bag. Leave to rest for 2 hours.

3 Meanwhile, start on the flavorings. Separate each head of garlic into cloves, leaving the skin on. Put into a pan, and add enough olive oil to cover the garlic, then heat gently until just the odd bubble breaks the surface. Cook over very low heat for about 10 to 15 minutes until soft and darkened, by which time they will have become very sweet. Leave to cool down a little in the pan, and then lift out the cloves, and squeeze the soft flesh from the skin of each clove into a small bowl, discarding the skin. Set aside.

4 Heat a little vegetable oil in a separate pan and fry the bacon cubes until light golden on all sides. Drain on paper towels and set aside.

5 To make the dough, transfer the ferment to a food mixer, add the water, and then the strong bread flour and salt. Roughly break the yeast on top on the opposite side of the bowl to the salt, and mix for 4 minutes on low speed, then turn up to medium for 10 to 12 minutes, until the dough comes away cleanly from the bowl.

MAKES 3 FOUGASSES

300g cool water
900g strong bread flour
20g sea salt
10g compressed fresh yeast
a little semolina flour, for dusting the peel

For the ferment:
100g rye flour
10g compressed fresh yeast
400g good ale

For the flavorings:
2 heads of garlic
a little olive oil
a little vegetable oil
250g bacon in one piece, cut into cubes
100g Gruyère cheese, grated, plus a little extra to sprinkle on the dough (optional)

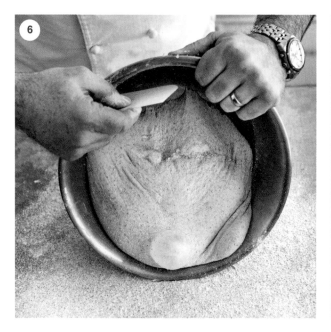

6 Turn out the dough using a scraper onto a lightly floured work surface, and also lightly flour a clean bowl.

7 Form the dough into a ball following steps 20 to 23 on pages 50 to 52, and leave to rest, covered, for about 45 minutes until just under double in size (see page 27).

8 Preheat the oven to 475°F and put in a baking stone or upturned baking pan to heat up.

9 Fill a clean spray bottle with water.

10 Lightly flour your work surface, and turn out the dough so that the top is now underneath.

11 Lightly flour the surface of the dough and, with your fingertips, gently prod it into a rough rectangle about 11 x 16 inches. Turn the dough so the long edge is facing you, and pile the bacon cubes, garlic, and Gruyère (if using) over the surface.

12 Fold one of the long sides into the center, over the filling, and then fold the other side over the top to create a parcel.

13 Using the flat edge of your scraper, cut the filled dough into three equal pieces.

14 Now use the flat edge of a scraper to make a series of cuts, slightly on the diagonal, all the way through—either in a single row or a double row—but make sure your cuts don't go all the way to the edges.

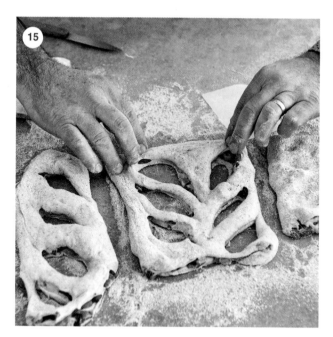

15 Open out the cuts a little with your fingers—if you made a single row of cuts, the strips will resemble a ladder. Scatter the surface of each fougasse with extra grated cheese, if you like.

16 Transfer the fougasses, one at a time, onto a lightly floured baking peel or pan, and then slide them quickly onto the hot baking stone or pan in the preheated oven. Just before you close the door, mist the inside of the oven using the water spray. Bake for 15 minutes, until dark golden. Allow to cool a little before eating.

Cornettis

These feature another dough that owes its depth of flavor to a simple flour, yeast, and water ferment. *Cornetti* is an Italian nickname for cow's udder, and you can see the resemblance, which is achieved by some clever folding of the dough —however, I always think the shaped rolls look more like the fingers of a hand, so I couldn't resist re-creating the famous photograph of Pablo Picasso, *Picasso and the Loaves*, which was taken by French photographer, Robert Doisneau, in a café in 1952. The folding of the dough (which is very stiff) is difficult to explain in words, so I suggest you watch the video online, where it will become clear. Alternatively, you can use the dough to make simpler shapes, as below.

**MAKES ABOUT
9 LARGE ROLLS**

300g cool water
900g strong bread flour
10g compressed fresh yeast
20g fine sea salt
150g extra virgin olive oil
a little semolina flour, for
   dusting the peel

For the ferment:
100g cool water
100g strong bread flour
10g compressed fresh yeast

1 Start by making the ferment: put the water, flour, and yeast into the bowl of your mixer. Mix on slow speed for about 3 to 4 minutes until you have a stiff dough. Cover with a freezer bag, large enough to cover the whole bowl, and leave at room temperature for at least 6 hours, but preferably overnight.

2 Add the water, flour, yeast, salt, and oil to the ferment, and mix on slow speed for 4 minutes, then increase the speed to medium for an additional 6 minutes. The dough will be quite tight and silky.

3 Cover the bowl with a large freezer bag as before, and leave to rest for 45 minutes (see page 27).

4 Don't flour the work surface, just turn out the dough with a scraper, so that the bottom of the dough is now on top.

5 Use the scraper to divide the dough into 9 x 190g pieces, and form each one into a ball following steps 20 to 23 on pages 50 to 52. Cover with a large freezer bag or baking cloth, and leave to rest again for an additional 10 minutes.

6 Preheat the oven to 475°F and put in a baking stone or an upturned baking pan to heat up. Fill a clean spray bottle with water.

7 To make long rolls, very lightly flour the work surface and roll out each ball of dough as thinly as possible into a long, thin oval shape (about 16 inches), using as little flour as possible; just enough to stop the dough sticking. Starting at the narrow end, roll up each oval loosely. To make round rolls, re-form each ball of dough into a tight ball.

Cornetti is an Italian nickname for cow's udder, and you can see the resemblance.

8 Place your rolls on a couche (see page 12), or baking pan and leave to rise for about 45 minutes.

9 Dust the baking peel (see page 14) with semolina flour, and transfer the rolls to the peel. Make a series of cuts across the top of each round roll with a lame (see page 14).

10 Slide the rolls onto the hot baking stone or pan in the preheated oven. Do this as quickly as possible to retain the heat. Just before you close the door, mist the inside of the oven using the water spray, avoiding getting water on the rolls themselves. Turn the heat down to 450°F.

11 Bake for 25 to 30 minutes, turning the heat down again to 400°F for the last 5 to 7 minutes, until light golden.

Spelt bread

The ancient grain of spelt has a slightly nutty flavor, and although it contains gluten, this is less "strong" than in the grains of its cousins in the wheat family, so people intolerant to wheat, might find this bread easier to digest. One day I had a call from Lydia and Toby Whatley of Toad's Mill, an enterprising young couple who grow a small production of beautiful spelt on their family farm in Herefordshire, which they stone-mill in batches; and now they have converted a horse trailer into a pop-up pizza restaurant, complete with wood-fired oven. I made some bread with their flour, and have been using it ever since. In the photograph, you can see the journey of their grain from field to flour: either whole-wheat (see middle left in the picture opposite), which is milled with none of the bran removed, or the finer "light white" flour, which is actually cream-colored white spelt. In the bread below I've used a mixture, together with some spelt flakes (rolled spelt grains) for additional texture.

I make these loaves in proving baskets, but you can just roughly shape the dough by hand, and leave the loaves to rise on a heavy baking cloth or couche. Spelt loaves tend to rise quicker than those made with wheat flour, so keep an eye on them; however you can slow the process down if you need to by putting them in the fridge for up to 2 hours.

MAKES 2 LARGE (900G) LOAVES

650g cold water
50g cold-pressed canola oil
600g white spelt flour
300g whole-wheat spelt flour
50g spelt flakes, plus extra for dusting (optional)
20g sea salt
15g compressed fresh yeast
a little semolina flour, for dusting the peel

For the ferment:
100 white spelt flour
100g warm water
5g compressed fresh yeast

---

1 Start by making the ferment. Put the flour in a bowl, break up the yeast and lightly rub it into the flour using the flat of your hands. Mix in the water, and then cover with a baking cloth or large freezer bag, and leave to rest for 4 hours. Alternatively, leave it for 2 hours, and then put it into the fridge overnight.

2 To make the dough, transfer the ferment to a food mixer, add the water, oil, the two spelt flours, the spelt flakes, and the salt. Break up the yeast roughly on top, on the opposite side of the bowl to the salt. Mix for 4 minutes on slow speed, then turn up to medium speed for about 8 to 10 minutes, until the dough comes away cleanly from the sides of the bowl.

3 Use your scraper to turn out the dough onto a lightly floured work surface, and also lightly flour a clean bowl.

4 Form the dough into a ball following steps 20 to 23 on pages 50 to 52, and leave to rest in the bowl, covered, for about 45 minutes, until just under double in size.

5 Re-form the dough into a ball as above, and leave to rest for an additional 30 minutes, covered with a baking cloth or a large freezer bag.

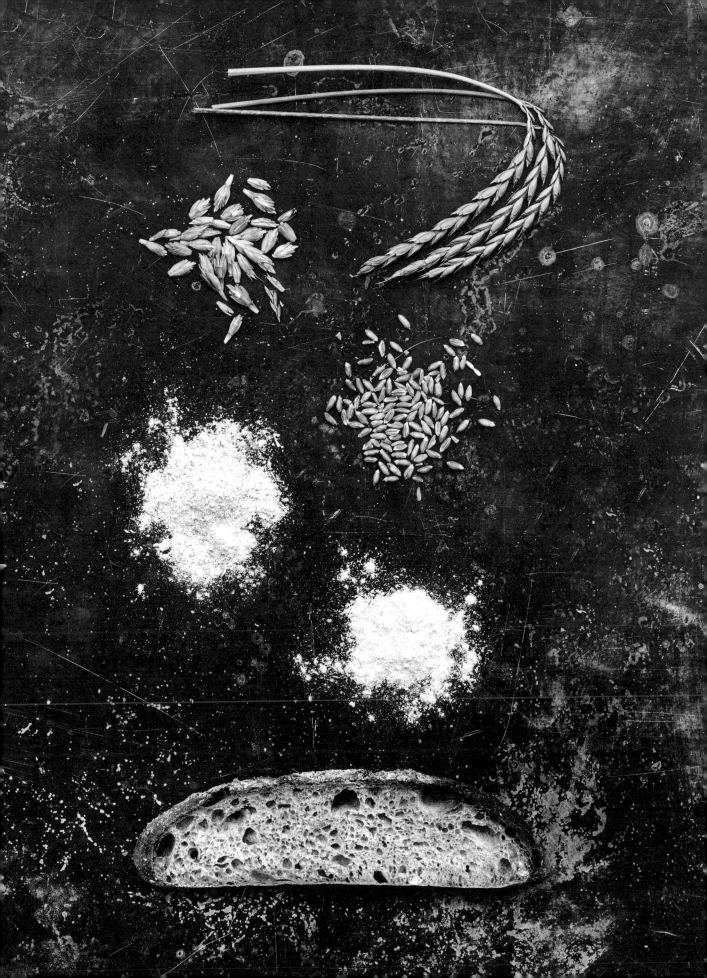

The ancient grain of spelt has a slightly nutty flavor, and although it contains gluten, this is less "strong" than in the grains of its cousins in the wheat family.

6 Flour your work surface, and turn out the dough with a scraper so that the bottom of the dough is now the top.

7 Divide the dough in half (see step 15 on page 64) and re-shape each piece into a quite loose ball as before. Cover and leave to rest for an additional 15 minutes.

8 Dust two proving baskets well with flour or spelt flakes.

9 Shape each ball of dough roughly according to the shape of your basket and put, top-side downwards, inside. Cover again and allow to rise for about 45 minutes, until just under double in size.

10 Preheat the oven to 475°F and put in a baking stone or upturned baking pan for a good hour to heat through thoroughly.

11 Lightly dust two peels or baking pans with semolina flour. Turn out the dough from each basket and place on a peel or pan so that the smooth top surface is facing upwards. Using your lame or the tip of a sharp serrated-edged knife, slash the top in a criss-cross fashion (or in your own pattern, if you prefer).

12 Slide the loaves onto the hot stones or baking pans. Just before closing the door, quickly mist the inside of the oven generously with your water spray, pumping it for a good 10 seconds, avoiding spraying the bread as much as possible.

13 Turn down the heat to 425°F for 20 minutes, and then turn down to 400°F for another 20 minutes, opening the door slightly, so that it is just ajar for the last 4 to 5 minutes, until the crust, where it has burst open, is a rich golden brown. Allow to cool completely on a wire rack before eating.

Apple and cider rolls

These rolls use a "soaker" (see page 59), made with barley flour, grains (pearl barley) and hard cider, which strengthens the dough, and boosts the flavor and keeping properties of the crumb. The rolls are baked with thin slivers of apple on top, which curl and brown a little around the edges, so they are quite fun to look at. They are great for breakfast, or to eat with cheese or rich pâté on a picnic—I take some with me on the rare occasions I can sneak away to my favorite spot on the River Avon for an hour or two of fishing.

MAKES ABOUT 12 SMALL ROLLS

230g barley flour
150g good-quality hard cider (dry or sweet)
30g pearl barley
200g cold water
300g strong white bread flour, plus extra for dusting
10g fine sea salt
15g compressed fresh yeast

For the topping:
3 eating apples
1 teaspoon ground cinnamon or pumpkin pie spice

---

1 Weigh off 30g of the barley flour into a large bowl.

2 Warm the cider in a pan until just simmering, then remove from the heat, and whisk into the barley flour. Leave to cool for 15 to 20 minutes.

3 Meanwhile, soak the pearl barley in enough warm water to cover for 5 minutes, then drain.

4 Transfer the flour and cider mixture to a food mixer, add the water and the soaked pearl barley, along with the rest of the barley flour, the strong white bread flour, and the salt. Roughly break up the yeast on top on the opposite side of the bowl to the salt, and mix for 4 minutes on low speed, then turn up to medium speed for 10 to 12 minutes, until the dough comes away cleanly from the sides of the bowl.

5 Turn out the dough using your scraper onto a lightly floured work surface, and also lightly flour a clean bowl.

6 Form the dough into a ball following steps 20 to 23 on pages 50 to 52, and leave to rest in the bowl, covered, for about 45 minutes to 1 hour, until just under double in size (see page 27).

7 Peel, core, and chop two of the apples into large dice, then toss in the cinnamon or pumpkin pie spice. Slice the third apple very finely, preferably using a mandoline.

8 Divide the dough into 12 pieces of about 80g each (see step 15 on page 64), and re-form into balls as above.

9 Turn the balls over, so that they are now top-side down, lightly flatten each one with your hand, and place 2 or 3 pieces of apple in the center. Close the dough over the apple, and turn the rolls over so that the seam is underneath. Place on a baking pan lined with parchment paper. Dust the tops lightly with flour, and press a slice of apple on top. Cover with a baking cloth or a large freezer bag, and allow to rise for about 1 hour, until just under double in size.

10 Preheat the oven to 450°F. Fill a clean spray bottle with water.

11 Put the pan into the preheated oven. Just before you close the door, quickly mist the inside of the oven generously with your water spray, pumping it for about 10 seconds, and avoiding spraying the rolls as much as possible. Bake for 15 to 20 minutes, until golden brown.

Oatmeal, honey, and raspberry loaves

I love this bread lightly toasted the day after it's made with fresh raspberries and goat milk yogurt for breakfast.

MAKES 2 MEDIUM LOAVES

50g rolled oats, plus extra for
  dusting and coating
100g goat milk
40g honey
300g cool water
450g strong white bread flour
10g fine sea salt
10g compressed fresh yeast
250g frozen raspberries
a little vegetable oil or butter,
  for greasing the pans

1 Bring the oats and milk to the boil in a pan. Stir in the honey, then remove from the heat, scrape into a bowl, and leave to cool.

2 To make the dough, transfer the oatmeal mixture to a food mixer, add the water, then the flour and salt, and roughly break up the yeast on top on the opposite side of the bowl to the salt. Mix for 4 minutes on slow speed, then turn up to medium for about an additional 12 minutes, until you have a dough that comes away cleanly from the sides of the bowl.

3 Lightly dust a work surface with oats, then turn out the dough. Also dust a clean bowl with oats. Add the raspberries to the dough, then form into a ball following steps 20 to 23 on pages 50 to 52, and rest for about 45 minutes to 1 hour, until just under double in size (see page 27).

4 Divide the dough in half using your scraper, and re-form each piece into a ball as above. Cover as before, and leave to rest for an additional 10 minutes.

5 Grease two medium loaf pans (8½ x 4½ inches) with oil or butter, and place on a baking pan. Have some more oats in a large shallow bowl. Brush the top and sides of each ball with water and dip into the oats to coat, then put into the loaf pans. Cover with a baking cloth or a large freezer bag and allow to rise for 45 minutes to 1 hour, until just under double in size.

6 Preheat the oven to 450°F. Fill a clean spray bottle with water. Using your lame or a sharp serrated-edged knife, make a cut along the length of each loaf, then put the pan into the preheated oven. Just before closing the door, quickly mist the inside generously with your water spray, pumping it for about 5 to 6 seconds, and avoiding spraying the loaves as much as possible.

7 Bake for about 15 to 20 minutes, then turn the heat down to 400°F for 10 minutes (leave the oven door very slightly ajar for the last 3 to 4 minutes to allow some steam to escape in order to enhance the crust) until the tops of the loaves are golden, and the oats are light brown.

Muesli breakfast bread

This recipe combines bread and cereal, so it is breakfast all in one! You can make it the day before you want to eat it and it will last for another 3 to 4 days. Be as creative as you like, adding whatever muesli, fruit and nuts are your favorite. I suggest you bake the bread "free-form" so that it looks quite rustic, but you could use pans as in the previous recipe for Oatmeal, Honey and Raspberry Loaves.

MAKES 2 SMALL LOAVES

200g water
250g strong white bread flour, plus extra for dusting
50g rye flour
10g fine sea salt
180g muesli mix of your choice
50g dried apricots, chopped
50g dried figs, chopped
50g dried apples, chopped
rolled oats, for coating

For the ferment:
200g strong whole-wheat flour
30g honey
15g compressed fresh yeast
200g water

1 Start by making the ferment. Combine whole-wheat flour, honey, yeast, and water in a large mixing bowl and leave for 2 hours until the mixture bubbles up, and is almost double in size.

2 To make the dough, transfer the ferment to a food mixer, add the water, white bread flour, and rye flour, and also the salt. Mix for 4 minutes on slow speed, then turn up to medium for about an additional 12 minutes, until you have a dough that comes away cleanly from the sides of the bowl. Add the muesli and dried fruit, and mix for no longer than 30 to 40 seconds on the lowest speed.

3 Turn out the dough using the scraper onto a lightly floured work surface, and also lightly flour a clean bowl.

4 Form the dough into a ball following steps 20 to 23 on pages 50 to 52. Leave to rest in the bowl, covered with a baking cloth or a large freezer bag, for 1 hour, until just under double in size (see page 27).

5 Turn out the dough onto a lightly floured work surface, and divide it in half, then re-form each piece of dough into a ball as above, slightly elongating into an oval shape.

6 Put the rolled oats in a large shallow bowl. Brush the top and sides of each loaf with water, and dip into the oats to coat.

7 Place on a baking pan, cover with a baking cloth or a large freezer bag, and allow to rise for 45 minutes to 1 hour, until just under double in size.

8 Preheat the oven to 450°F. Fill a clean spray bottle with water.

9 Put the pan into the preheated oven. Just before closing the door, quickly mist the inside generously with your water spray, pumping it for about 10 seconds, and avoiding spraying the bread as much as possible. Turn the heat down to 400°F for 25 to 30 minutes, until the top of the bread and the oats are light brown.

White sourdough

Patience is something that doesn't seem to come naturally to most human beings, but you need plenty of it if you are going to make good sourdough, since it will take you a minimum of five days to develop the ferment and to make your first loaf. Think of yeast as a time machine. If you use fresh commercial yeast, the more you add—especially dried yeast—the quicker the dough will rise during resting and rising, but the baked bread will become stale and, if you use too much yeast, it could become less digestible. When you work with natural yeasts, as in sourdough, these take much longer to develop, so the dough will take longer to rise, but the bread will be much more digestible. From the moment you bite into the thick, crunchy crust, and begin chewing, you will get the saliva going, which starts breaking down the carbs and proteins, and the "friendly" lactic acid bacteria (which gives sourdough its characteristic tangy flavor) help to keep a good balance of flora in the gastrointestinal tract.

As mentioned previously, I prefer to use plastic containers for making and storing the ferment, rather than glass, as there is always the danger that it might break. You will need two proving baskets.

STAGE 1:
100g strong white bread flour
100g warm water
20g honey

Mix all the ingredients together in a large plastic container, cover with a freezer bag, large enough to cover the entire container, and leave in a warm place for 24 to 36 hours, without disturbing it. The mixture will start to smell a little alcoholic, darken in color, and bubbles will begin to form (see page 93). These are signs that fermentation is underway, and you can move on to stage 2.

STAGE 2:
100g strong white bread flour
200g warm water

Add the flour and water to your ferment, mix well, cover as before, and leave in a warm place for an additional 24 to 36 hours. At the end of this stage, the mixture will have expanded a little, and be starting to smell sweet and lightly fermented (see page 93). Time to move on to stage 3.

STAGE 3:
100g strong white bread flour
200g warm water

Add the flour and water to your ferment, mix well, cover as before, and leave in a warm place for an additional 24 to 36 hours.

By the end of this stage, you should have a total of 800g of ferment. Use half of this to make your bread, and keep the rest in the fridge to make another batch of bread (see page 94 for how to refresh your ferment and keep it going).

1 Put the ferment into a large mixing bowl, add the flour and salt, then pour in the water and follow steps 5 to 23 on pages 39 to 52. Leave to rest for 45 minutes, until just under double in size (see page 27).

2 Turn out the dough and re-form into a ball (see steps 20 to 23 on pages 50 to 52), then cover, and leave to rest for an additional 45 minutes.

3 Divide the dough in two (see step 15 on page 64) and re-form each piece into quite a loose ball as before. Cover with a baking cloth or a large freezer bag, and leave to rest for an additional 15 minutes.

4 Dust your proving baskets well with flour (see opposite).

5 Shape each ball of dough roughly according to the shape of your basket, and place, top-side downwards, inside.

6 Cover again, and allow to rise for 4 to 6 hours, until just under double in size. Alternatively you can let the dough rise for 3 hours, and then put the baskets in the fridge overnight. Bring them out an hour before you want to bake.

7 Preheat the oven to 475°F, then put in a baking stone or upturned tray to warm up for an hour. Fill a clean spray bottle with water.

8 Lightly dust a peel or baking pan with semolina flour. Turn out the dough from each basket onto the peel or pan, keeping it the same way up. Using your lame, or the tip of a sharp knife, slash the top in criss-cross fashion (or as you like).

9 Slide the loaves onto your hot stone or baking tray. Just before closing the oven door, quickly mist the inside generously with the water spray, pumping it for a good 10 seconds, avoiding spraying the bread as much as possible.

10 Bake for 5–6 minutes, then turn the heat down to 425°F for 20 minutes. Turn the temperature down again to 400°F for an additional 5 minutes, then open the door slightly so that it is just ajar for a final 2 to 3 minutes, until the "burst" of the crust is a rich golden brown. Allow the loaves to cool completely before eating.

MAKES 2 LARGE LOAVES

400g ferment (see page 91)
1kg strong white bread flour, plus extra for dusting
20g fine sea salt
700g water
a little semolina flour, for dusting the peel or baking pan

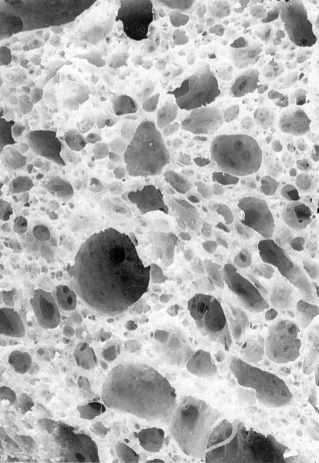

Keeping your ferment going

REFRESHING

Once you have made a first ferment, and used half of it to make sourdough, you need to refresh the rest. Refreshing means mixing the ferment with flour and water in order to keep it alive, and how often you do this depends on how regularly you want to bake.

THE FORMULA

The process of refreshing is very straightforward: simply weigh the ferment, then mix it with half the quantity of both water and strong bread flour. If, for example, you have followed the recipe for white sourdough on page 91, you will have used 400g of ferment to make bread and kept back the remaining 400g. To this you add 200g water and 200g strong bread flour. Mix until all the flour has disappeared, then cover the bowl with a large freezer bag, and put it into the fridge. The mixture will continue fermenting and slowly expanding, and after 2 to 3 days, you will have about 800g of ferment: 400g to make your next batch of bread, and 400g to keep back to refresh again. In this way, you can maintain a continuous process of baking and refreshing.

QUICKER

If you want to make another batch of bread in less than two days, you can accelerate the process. Once you have mixed your ferment with water and flour, leave it at room temperature for at least 6 to 8 hours, then you can use it within 12 hours. It is ready when it has the stretchy honeycomb texture pictured opposite, and a sweet, lactic smell.

SLOWER

If you only want to bake every week or so, then you need to slow things down, and just refresh your ferment every 4 to 5 days, otherwise it will start to take over your fridge. Just keep an eye on it. When all is going well, it will have the sweet smell and texture described above. If you do find that you have too much ferment, and don't have time to make bread, don't waste it, as you can use the ferment just as it is to make the sourdough crackers on page 96.

TROUBLESHOOTING

If the ferment is becoming dormant—i.e., it will seem hard and dense, and will be losing its smell— it is probably too cold for it to be properly active, s take it out of the fridge for 12 to 24 hours to bring it back to life, and then return it to the fridge. On the other hand, if the ferment is beginning to smell too pungent, overripe and vinegary, and if the crusty top is very discolored, and/or there is a wateriness about the texture, this shows that it is going too quickly and is on the turn. You can still save it by scraping off the top until you get to the center, which should still smell pleasant, and look like honeycomb. Re-weigh it, and refresh it as usual by mixing it with half the quantity of water and strong bread flour. Return it to the fridge, and you should be back on course.

HOLIDAYS

Unless you are going away for more than two or three weeks, you don't need a babysitter for your ferment. The trick is to increase the volume of your ferment before you go away by adding twice the usual ratio of water and flour, because the greater the volume, the slower the ferment will mature, and the longer it can go before it needs refreshing. So, before you go on holiday, weigh 400g of ferment as usual, but add 400g of water and 400g of strong bread flour. This will give you enough ferment to last for 2 to 3 weeks while you are away. When you return, you can just skim off the thick layer on top and discard it to get to the heart of the ferment which should still be active, with a good honeycomb texture and lactic smell. Then you can get back to the usual routine of weighing the ferment that is left, and refreshing it.

DON'T FORGET

You can experiment with most of the yeasted recipes in this book by substituting some of the fresh commercial yeast with some ferment, in a ratio of 10g of ferment to 1g of fresh commercial yeast. So if a recipe calls for 20g compressed fresh yeast, try just using 10g and adding 100g of ferment, then, as you feel more confident, you can keep increasing the quantity of ferment until eventually you might choose to use no fresh commercial yeast at all

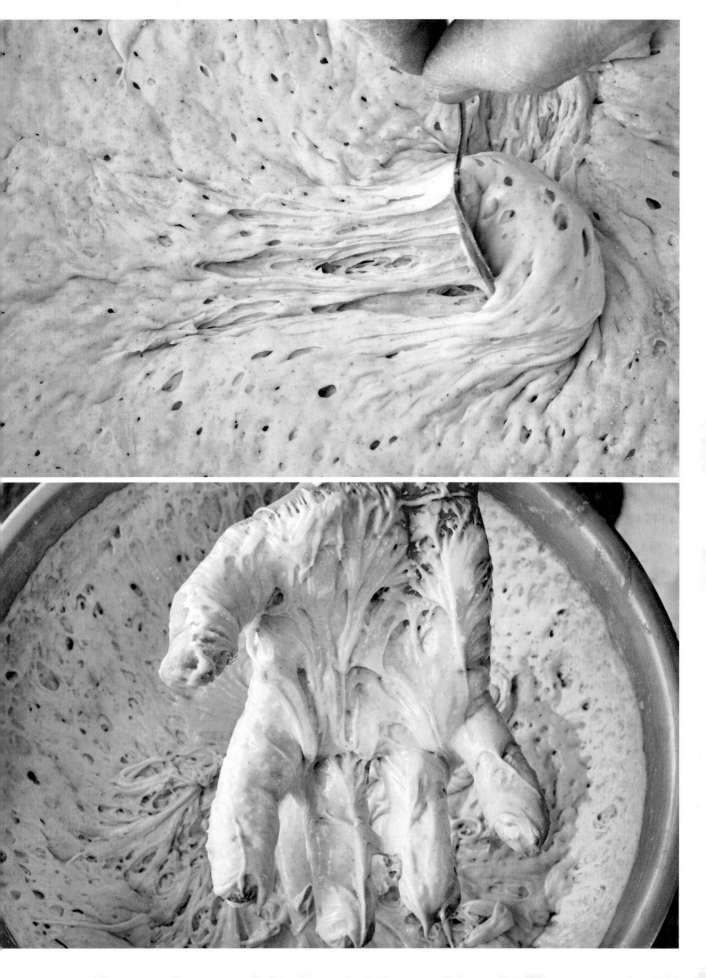

Sourdough crackers

These are really simple to make, and a great way of using up any white or rye sourdough ferment that you don't use to make bread. There is no resting or rising involved. All you need to do is add enough flour to the sourdough ferment to lose the stickiness, and make it malleable, then roll out into rounds. I like to stamp a hole into the center of each cracker, and then stack them on a wooden baton to serve. Once crisply baked, the crackers should keep well for a few weeks in an airtight container.

MAKES 8

200g any sourdough ferment (see pages 91, 102 and 104)
sea salt flakes (optional)
a little strong white bread flour or rye flour, for dusting the work surface
a little semolina flour, for dusting the peels

1 Place the ferment in a bowl and mix in enough flour to make a stiff enough dough to roll into a log. Cut into eight pieces.

2 Place a baking stone or an upturned heavy baking pan in the oven and preheat to 400°F.

3 Flour the work surface well, and press the first piece of dough into the flour, turning it over a few times so that it is well dusted.

4 Roll it out into a rough round about 4 to 4¾ inches in diameter, adding a little more flour if necessary to prevent sticking. Repeat with the other pieces of dough.

5 Have a peel or flat baking sheet ready.

6 If you want to neaten the crackers, use a large cutter to trim off the edges, and then a small cutter to stamp out a hole in the middle. Bake these for 3 to 4 minutes. (At this point you can also gently press some flakes of sea salt into each cracker—or just leave them plain).

7 Transfer the crackers to your loading peel and slide them onto the baking stone or pan. Bake for 5 to 6 minutes, until the crackers have puffed up very slightly, and are crisp.

Sourdough pizza

The recipe here is for a classic Margherita topping: a simple affair of tomato, mozzarella, and basil, but you can add whatever ingredients you like. When I am at home with the kids, I flatten out the rounds of dough and then have little mounds of ingredients, such as sliced mushrooms, thin slivers of chorizo or prosciutto and I give them what they want. Ham is also good added when the pizza comes out of the oven. If you prefer a "white" pizza without the tomato purée, spread a dollop of crème fraîche over the dough instead, and add some crabmeat or smoked salmon before the pizza goes into the oven. Serve with arugula and a squeeze of lemon juice.

The dough also makes excellent flatbread if you simply bake it brushed with a little olive oil and sea salt and black pepper—or you can add a sprinkling of ground cumin, if you like.

MAKES 4 MEDIUM PIZZAS ABOUT 12 INCHES

½ quantity of white sourdough dough (see pages 91 to 92) made as far as the end of step 2
200g tomato purée
200g good mozzarella, torn into pieces
handful of fresh basil leaves
extra virgin olive oil, for drizzling
sea salt and freshly ground black pepper
a little semolina or all-purpose flour, for dusting the peel

1 Divide the dough into four and roll each ball of dough in a little semolina or flour, place on a baking pan, and cover with a baking cloth or a large freezer bag. Leave to rest for 1 hour. Alternatively leave overnight in the fridge.

2 Preheat the oven to 500°F, or as hot as your oven will go, and put in a baking stone or upturned baking pan. Remember, if you are using a baking stone, it will need an hour to heat up.

3 Flour the work surface well, then take a piece of dough and roll it out into a rough round about 12 inches in diameter, turning the dough over a few times in between rolls.

4 Depending on the size of your oven, bake one or two pizzas at a time. Lightly dust one or two peels or baking sheets with semolina flour, and lay a circle of dough on top.

5 Spread a ladleful of tomato purée over the dough, taking care not to spill any on the peel, or it might stop the pizza from sliding off smoothly into the oven.

6 Add some pieces of mozzarella, and scatter over some basil leaves, then drizzle a little olive oil over the top and season.

7 Slide each pizza onto the baking stone or sheet in the preheated oven, and bake them for them one at a time for 8 to 10 minutes, depending on your oven, and how crisp and golden you like your pizza.

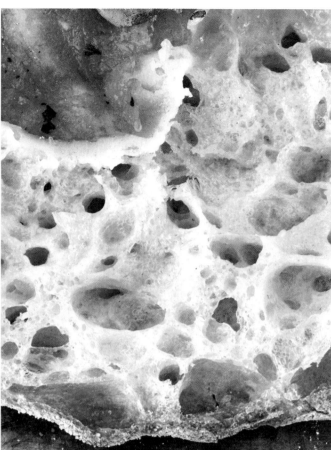

Quinoa bread

You can use a sourdough ferment not only to go on to make a sourdough loaf, but to combine with some compressed fresh yeast if you want to make a quicker bread, but with a crumb that has the depth of flavor and texture of sourdough.

MAKES 2 MEDIUM (400G) PAN LOAVES OR 8 VERY SMALL (100G) ONES

100g quinoa
30g coconut oil
1 small floury potato
150g white sourdough ferment
  (see page 91)
150g whole-wheat flour
50g malted wheat flakes
50g honey
100g cold water
200g strong white bread flour
10g fine sea salt
20g compressed fresh yeast
a little oil or butter for
  greasing the pans

1 Cook the quinoa in 250g boiling water for about 15 minutes, until all of the water has been absorbed, and the quinoa is just tender. While it is still warm, stir in the coconut oil.

2 Meanwhile peel and dice the potato, and add to a pan containing 200g cold salted water. Bring to a boil, and cook until soft when pierced with the tip of a knife. Don't drain the potato pieces, but mash them in the pan. Stir in the quinoa and coconut oil mixture, and leave to cool for about 15 minutes.

3 In a large mixing bowl, combine the quinoa and mashed potato mixture with the ferment, whole-wheat flour, wheat flakes, and honey. Cover with a baking cloth or large freezer bag, and leave to rest for 30 minutes.

4 To make the dough, transfer the mixture to a food mixer, add the 100g cold water, then the strong white bread flour and the salt, and roughly break up the yeast on top on the opposite side of the bowl to the salt. Mix for 4 minutes on slow speed, then turn up to medium for about an additional 12 minutes, until you have a dough that comes away cleanly from the sides of the bowl. Form the dough into a ball following steps 20 to 23 on pages 50 to 52, place in a clean bowl, cover, and leave to rest for about 30 minutes, until just under double in size (see page 27).

5 Re-form the dough into a ball as above, and rest again for an additional 30 minutes.

6 Preheat the oven to 400°F, grease your pans with oil or butter, and place on a baking sheet.

7 Divide the dough in half or into four, following step 15 on page 64. Form the pieces into balls as above, and place in the prepared pans. Cover, and allow to rise for 1–1½ hours.

8 Put the baking sheet into the preheated oven, and bake for 20 minutes for very small loaves, or 30 minutes for larger ones, until golden. Cool slightly, then turn out.

Malted wheat sourdough

This is made in the same way as the White sourdough on pages 91 to 93, but with a rye and ale ferment, and a malted wheat flake soaker. The additional natural yeast in the ale lightens the texture and flavor. You will need two proving baskets.

STAGE 1:
100g strong white bread flour
50g rye flour
80g stout or porter, warmed in a pan (just enough to take the chill off)

Mix the ingredients together in a large plastic container, cover with a freezer bag large enough to cover the entire container, and leave in a warm place for 24 hours, without disturbing it.

STAGE 2:
250g strong white bread flour
50g rye flour
100g stout or porter, warmed in a pan
100g warm water

Add the ingredients to your ferment, mix well, cover as before, and leave in a warm place for an additional 24 hours.

STAGE 3:
200g strong white bread flour
200g warm water

Add the ingredients to your ferment, mix well, cover as before, and leave in a warm place for 12 hours.
  At the end of this stage you should have a total of 1.130kg of ferment. Weigh 500g for your bread, and keep the rest to make your next batch (see page 94 for how to refresh your ferment and keep it going).

1 At least 2 hours before you are ready to bake (or the day before), make the soaker. Put the malted wheat flakes in a bowl, pour over the water, mix well, and set aside.

2 Put the soaker in a large mixing bowl with the ferment and the rest of the ingredients, then follow steps 1 to 9 on page 92 for White sourdough (but don't divide the dough in two).

3 Bake for 5 to 6 minutes, then turn the heat down to 450°F for 10 minutes. Turn the heat down again to 400°F for an additional 15 minutes, then open the door slightly, so that it is just ajar for the final 5 minutes, until the "burst" of the crust is a rich golden brown. Allow to cool completely on a wire rack before eating.

MAKES 2 LARGE LOAVES

For the sourdough:
500g ferment (see above)
500g strong white bread flour
350g malted wheat flour
50g rye flour
20g fine sea salt
225g water
225g stout or porter

For the soaker:
200g malted wheat flakes
350g water

100 percent rye sourdough

Rye is a grain that I find people tend to love or hate. Personally I love it, and I use it frequently in my breadmaking. If you like your sourdough with a crumb that is really dense, earthy, and sour, then this is the one for you. The rye makes for a very sticky dough that is difficult to work by hand, so use a mixer. You will need two medium-sized proving baskets or one large one.
The quantities for the ferment and the recipe that follows can both be easily halved if you want to make a smaller amount of ferment to start off with, or just want to bake one loaf instead of two.

STAGE 1:
100g dark rye flour
10g dark brown sugar
200g warm water

Mix the ingredients together in a large plastic container, cover with a freezer bag large enough to cover the entire container, and leave in a warm place for 24 hours.

STAGE 2:
100g dark rye flour
200g warm water

Add all the ingredients to your ferment, mix well, cover as above, and leave in a warm place for an additional 24 hours.

STAGE 3:
100g dark rye flour
200g warm water

Add the ingredients to your ferment, mix well, cover as above, and leave in a warm place for 12 hours.

At the end of this stage, you should have a total of 900g of bubbly active ferment. Weigh 400g for your bread, and keep the rest to make your next batch of bread (see page 94 for how to refresh your ferment and keep it going).

1 Combine the ingredients for the soaker in the bowl of a mixer, and leave to cool.

2 To make the dough, add the rest of the ingredients, and mix on slow speed for 8 minutes. The dough will be very sticky, but don't worry about this.

3 Dust your work surface liberally with rye flour, then turn out the dough with the help of a scraper. Dust your proving baskets with rye flour, too.

4 Divide the dough in two, and without forming into a ball, just transfer each piece of dough to a basket. Cover, and leave to rise for 4 to 6 hours, until just under double in size (see page 27). Because the dough is so dense, it will crack, as shown in the picture on page 102.

MAKES 2 LARGE LOAVES

400g rye ferment
300g cold water
800g dark rye flour, plus extra
  for dusting
25g salt

For the soaker:
100g dark rye flour
100g boiling water

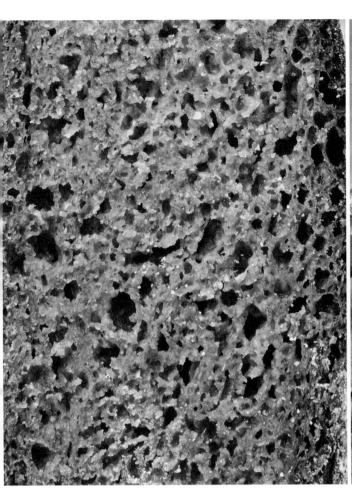

5 Preheat the oven to 425°F, and put in your baking stone or upside down pan to throughly heat through.

6 Dust two peels or flat baking sheets with semolina, and fill a clean spray bottle with water.

7 Turn the loaves out of the baskets onto the peels, and then slide them into the oven. Quickly mist the inside generously with your water spray, pumping it for a good 10 seconds, avoiding spraying the bread as much as possible.

8 Bake for 5–6 minutes, then turn the heat down to 400°F and bake for an additional 30 to 40 minutes. Allow to cool completely on a wire rack before eating.

Rustic miche

The name "miche" comes from the latin *mica*, which, like the French *mie*, means crumb. This method combines a sourdough ferment (I like to use a rye ferment) with a little fresh commercial yeast.

---

1 Put the ferment into a large mixing bowl and add the rest of the ingredients. Follow steps 1 to 3 for White sourdough on page 92. Reshape the dough into a ball, cover, and leave to rest for an additional 45 minutes.

2 Turn the dough over onto a lightly floured work surface so the top is facing downwards. Prod into a rough square, fold one corner into the center, and bring the opposite corner over the top. Repeat with the other two corners and turn over. Lift onto a well-floured couche, and leave to rise for 1½ to 2 hours, until just under double in size.

3 Preheat the oven to 475°F, and dust a loading peel with semolina. Turn the miche over onto the peel, and transfer to the oven for 5 to 6 minutes, misting the inside of the oven as you do so (see page 105), then turn the heat down to just over 400°F for 15 minutes. Turn down again to 400°F for another 10 minutes, then open the door so that it is just ajar for the final 4 to 5 minutes, until the crust, where it has burst open, is a rich golden brown. Allow to cool completely.

MAKES 1 LARGE MICHE

Either: 100g rye sourdough
  ferment (see page 104) or
  white sourdough ferment
  (see page 91)
400g strong white bread flour,
  plus extra for dusting
50g dark rye flour
50g whole-wheat or spelt flour
10g salt
350g water
5g compressed fresh yeast
a little semolina flour, for

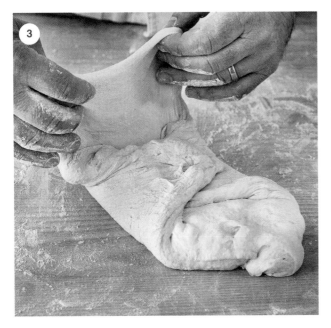

Enriched

Gotchial

Multicolored buns

Brie in brioche

Plum tart

Petits pains with Gruyère

English muffins

Pain de mie

Leopard bread

Chocolate, pistachio, and orange loaf

Kouign amann

Toasted pine nut, honey, and pear croustades

Almond and cherry slices or rolls

Cinnamon knots

Cheese twists

Salted caramel brioches

Caramelized apple and calvados brioche

Rum and golden raisin brioches

Challah

Russian braid

Panettone

When you add rich ingredients, such as eggs, milk, butter, and sugar (or honey, which I often like to use) to the essential mix of flour, yeast, salt, and water, the result is a dough that will give the finished bread a completely different, altogether silkier texture that can be almost melting. I hesitate to call these breads brioche, although they are all the same "family," because people tend to think of brioche as something sweet, whereas the flavor and crumb will vary according to the ratio of the enriching ingredients (like *pain de mie* and leopard bread), which goes very well with savory ingredients such as hams, pâtés and smoked fish.

Where one dough can be used in many different ways, I have grouped the recipes together. Although all the doughs can be mixed by hand (in which case follow steps 1 to 17 on pages 38 to 49, it can be hard work to incorporate the additional ingredients, so I recommend using a mixer, which will bring the ingredients together more efficiently, and the result is usually a lighter, more open crumb.

With enriched doughs, adding ingredients to the bowl is always the same: liquids, such as milk, eggs, honey, etc, go in first, then the flour (and salt if using), and sugar, with the yeast broken up on top. Keep both the salt and sugar out of direct contact with the yeast. As mentioned previously, salt can kill the yeast by sucking the moisture from it, but sugar is even more lethal as it caramelizes the yeast, forcing it to over-accelerate its action.

If the recipe only calls for a little butter—80g or less—you can just break this up and add it on top. Start the mixer off on low speed for 4 minutes, then turn it up to medium for about 10 to 15 minutes, depending on the recipe, until the dough comes away cleanly from the sides of the bowl. Don't be tempted to hurry things along by increasing the speed to high. Be patient.

At one end of the brioche scale is something ultra-rich (such as *Kouign amann* or panettone) and at the other a light bread with only a hint of sweetness.

If a dough recipe calls for more than 80g butter, leave it in the fridge until just before you start mixing, then place it between two sheets of waxed paper, and bash it with the end of a rolling pin to soften and soften and break it up into small pieces. Wait until you have turned up the mixer speed to medium before adding it, bit by bit.

With most of the recipes in this chapter, if you don't want to use the dough immediately, you can leave it to rest in a bowl covered with a large freezer bag in the fridge overnight, which will further develop the quality of the crumb, as well as the flavor. When you take it out of the fridge, it will feel quite solid because of the butter content, but don't worry, this is normal.

Gotchial

Gotchial is the name for a style of enriched dough made with crème fraîche, which is typical in Morbihan, the department of Brittany where I grew up. The cream is brought to a boil first, and the paste it forms with the flour helps to create a very light crumb, which stays fresher for longer. At one time, the use of butter and sugar meant it was an expensive treat, so it tended to be eaten only on Sundays and special occasions. I love it for breakfast, or in the afternoon with butter and good jam. For variety, you can add some chocolate chips or golden raisins to the dough, if you like, once the dough is ready. Incorporate them on low speed for a minute at the most.

MAKES 2 ROUND LOAVES

150g crème fraîche
500g strong white bread flour
125g cold unsalted butter
4 large eggs
25g compressed fresh yeast
125g superfine sugar
10g fine sea salt
vegetable oil or nonstick
  spray, for greasing

For the glaze:
1 egg
pinch of fine sea salt

1 Put the crème fraîche in a pan and bring to a boil, then remove from the heat immediately. Whisk in 50g of the flour, and allow to cool.

2 Place the cold butter between two sheets of waxed paper, and bash it with the end of a rolling pin to soften and break it up into small pieces.

3 Transfer the crème fraîche and flour mixture to the bowl of a food mixer, and add the eggs, then add the rest of the flour. Break up the compressed fresh yeast, and add to one side of the bowl. Add the sugar and salt on the other side of the bowl. Mix on slow speed for 4 minutes.

4 Increase the speed to medium, and after 2 minutes, add the butter, piece by piece, continuing to mix for about 10 to 12 minutes, until all the butter is incorporated, and the dough comes away cleanly from the sides of the bowl.

5 Lightly flour the work surface, and also a clean bowl. Use a scraper to turn out the dough onto the work surface.

6 Form the dough into a ball following steps 20 to 23 on pages 50 to 52, and leave to rest in the bowl for about 45 minutes, until just under double in size (see page 27).

7 Line two baking sheets with parchment paper, or grease them lightly with vegetable oil or nonstick spray.

8 Divide the dough in half widthwise, and form each half into a tight ball as before, then place on the prepared baking sheets. Cover with a baking cloth or a large freezer bag, and leave to rise for 1½ to 2 hours, until just under double in size.

9 While the dough is rising, beat the egg with the salt for the glaze.

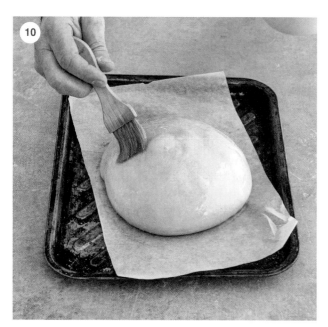

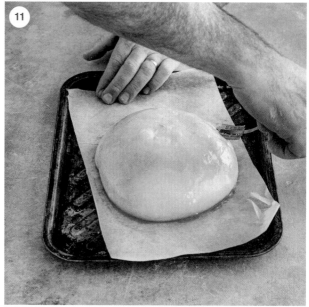

10 Preheat the oven to 375°F. Brush the top of each gotchial with the egg glaze.

11 With your lame (see page 14), or the tip of a sharp serrated-edged knife, make a cut all the way around the outside of each loaf. Do this as cleanly as possible, so that you don't drag the dough. This will allow the gotchial to burst, giving a dramatic contrast between the glazed and unglazed areas of the finished bread.

12 Put into the preheated oven, turn down the heat to 350°F, and bake for about 30 minutes, until the loaves look like rich, shiny brown chestnuts. Allow to cool completely on a wire rack before eating.

Multicolored buns

This recipe produces buns that are at the lightest end of the enriched spectrum. They are not too sweet, so they work well with savory fillings, even burgers. Commercially made burger buns can often be either quite dry in texture, or cloying, whereas these have a bite, but the crumb has quite a moist and melting quality, which means they are good toasted. The buns freeze well, so it is worth making plenty. Or double the quantity and use the rest to make the Brie in brioche recipe on page 122.

Have fun with different colors and flavorings: bright yellow buns made with turmeric, more subtly golden saffron ones flecked with seaweed, and—most dramatic looking of all—volcanic lava-like black buns, colored with charcoal bamboo powder, which I used for the first time when in Thailand. The charcoal is made by burning bamboo at very high temperature, and the powder, which is incredibly versatile, is used in everything from food coloring to face masks, and even for whitening teeth.

You can fill the buns with anything you like, but the flavor of both the turmeric version and the saffron and seaweed ones, is especially good with grilled fish, or even fish fingers. The black buns are great filled with fresh tuna steak, seared on a lightly oiled grill pan for a minute on each side. I like to add a layer of interesting salad leaves or micro herbs, and a spoonful of wasabi dressing—mix wasabi and some good mayonnaise, half and half, or less wasabi, depending on how much heat you can take.

Of course you can use this recipe to make plain buns—in which case, omit the charcoal, turmeric or saffron, and seaweed.

MAKES 16 BUNS

200g whole milk
3 large eggs
500g strong white bread flour, plus extra for dusting
20g compressed fresh yeast
60g superfine sugar
10g fine sea salt
50g cold unsalted butter

Variations:
either 10g black bamboo charcoal powder
or 2 teaspoons ground turmeric
or about 15 threads of saffron and 2 tablespoons dried seaweed flakes

For the glaze:
2 eggs
pinch of fine sea salt
1 tablespoon milk

sesame seeds, to decorate (optional)

The black buns are great
filled with fresh tuna steak,
seared on a lightly oiled grill
pan for a minute each side.

1 If making saffron and seaweed rolls, warm a little of the milk first, add the saffron threads, and leave to infuse for about 30 minutes.

2 Put the milk (or bamboo or turmeric powder-infused milk) and eggs into the bowl of a food mixer, then add the flour (and seaweed, if using). Break up the compressed fresh yeast and add to one side of the bowl. Add the sugar and salt on the other side of the bowl. Break the butter into pieces on top.

3 Mix on slow speed for 4 minutes, then increase the speed to medium, and continue to mix for about 12 to 15 minutes, until the dough comes away cleanly from the sides of the bowl.

4 Lightly flour the work surface, and a clean bowl. Use a scraper to turn the dough onto the work surface.

5 Form the dough into a ball following steps 20 to 23 on pages 50 to 52, and leave to rest in the bowl for about 1 hour, until just under double in size (see page 27).

6 Have ready two nonstick baking sheets, or line two sheets with parchment paper.

7 Divide the dough into 16 pieces of 60g each, and re-form into tight balls as above.

8 Place on the baking sheets, spaced well apart, cover with a baking cloth or a large freezer bag, and allow to rise for about 1 to 1¼ hours, until just under double in size.

9 While the buns are rising, preheat the oven to 375°F and beat the eggs with the salt in a small bowl for the glaze.

10 Once the buns have risen, beat the milk into the egg and salt mixture, and brush the top of each bun with this glaze. Sprinkle with sesame seeds, if you like.

11 Put the baking sheets into the preheated oven, turn down the heat to 350°F, and bake for about 15 minutes, until a shiny crust forms on the top of the rolls. Leave to cool before eating.

Brie in brioche

I love to make this for lunch for the family or friends, using the dough recipe on page 119, but without the flavorings. In France it is quite usual to serve a light brioche with something savory like cheese, liver pâté, or smoked salmon, but when we make this in my bread classes, it is often quite a revelation, and always a big favorite when we sit down and tuck into it at lunchtime.

Turn it into a bit of a party piece by serving some charcuterie on a separate board, and putting out a bowl of warm new potatoes, which everyone can use to scoop out all the cheese first, like a fondue. When the cheese has gone, I make a big green salad in a bowl, toss it with plenty of vinaigrette (made with 1 to 2 parts wine vinegar to 3 to 4 parts extra virgin olive oil and 1 teaspoon Dijon mustard, seasoned with sea salt and freshly ground black pepper), and some chopped walnuts, and tip it into the space left by the cheese. I then cut a big wedge for everyone to enjoy a fantastic mix of cheesy, herby, garlicky bread and salad.

If you buy a 1kg brie, this will feed 8 to 10. I may be French, but because it's good to support regional produce, I use a nice ripe English Somerset brie—but not so overripe that it is running over the table!

SERVES 8 TO 10

1 quantity of Multicolored buns dough (see page 119), omitting the flavorings
strong white bread flour, for dusting
1 large (1kg) ripe brie
2 garlic cloves, peeled, and finely sliced
a few small sprigs of fresh rosemary and thyme
2 tablespoons good extra virgin olive oil
dash of Pernod (optional)

For the glaze:
2 eggs
pinch of fine sea salt

1 Make the dough following steps 1 to 5 on page 121.

2 When the dough has rested, lightly flour your work surface and roll the dough into a rough circle.

3 Place a large baking ring (about 12 inches in diameter) on top of a baking sheet, then press in a large sheet of parchment paper.

4 Lower the dough into the paper, and use your fingertips to gently press it down in the center, and outwards into the shape of the ring, so that you create an indent big enough to hold the brie, while forming a rim around the outside of the cheese.

5 Put in the brie, and score the surface with a sharp knife in criss-cross fashion.

6 Push the slices of garlic into the cuts that you have made, along with the sprigs of fresh rosemary and thyme. Drizzle the whole thing with the olive oil. I like to sprinkle over a tablespoon of Pernod too, but that is up to you.

7 Cover with a large freezer bag and leave to rise for about 45 minutes (see page 27). During this time the rim of the dough will almost double in size.

8 While the dough is rising, preheat the oven to 375°F, and beat the eggs with the salt for the glaze.

9 Brush the rim of the dough with the egg glaze, and transfer the baking sheet to the preheated oven. Turn down the heat to 350°F, and bake for about 30 to 40 minutes, until the cheese has melted, and the rim of the brioche is a dark golden brown. If you lift up the parchment paper carefully, you should be able to see through it to check that the base of the brioche is also dark golden brown.

10 Remove from the oven, and holding the parchment paper, lift the brioche from the ring onto a board, and invite everyone to tuck in while it is still warm.

Plum tart

As a change from using flaky pastry for a fruit tart, I like to use an enriched dough, which gives the dessert a different quality: soft and unctuous. In this recipe I have combined two of my favorite creams: *crème pâtissière* and *crème d'amande* (almond), which, mixed together, I think are quite wonderful. However, you can use just one or the other, if you prefer, and double the quantity. I usually add a dash of alcohol when making almond cream, and for this recipe I use vanilla vodka. At the school, as well as storing any washed and dried vanilla beans that have been used to flavor creams in a jar of sugar, I put some of them into a bottle of vodka that we keep in the freezer. I have been doing this for about 12 years, so we now have a bottle of aged vanilla vodka, which looks quite extraordinary as it is stacked full of pods, and it tastes amazing.

---

1 First make the almond cream. Beat the butter in a bowl with a wooden spoon until pale and creamy, then add the sugar, and beat well until fluffy. Beat in the ground almonds, then the flour, and the egg, and finally stir in the alcohol. Put into the fridge for 15 minutes.

2 Make the *crème pâtissière* following steps 1 to 5 on page 177, but omitting the chocolate.

3 To make the dough, put the milk and eggs into the bowl of a food mixer, then add the flour. Break up the compressed fresh yeast, and add to one side of the bowl. Add the sugar and salt on the other side of the bowl to the yeast. Break up the butter on top. Mix on slow speed for 4 minutes, then increase the speed to medium for about 10 to 12 minutes, until the dough comes cleanly away from the sides of the bowl.

4 Lightly flour the work surface, and also a clean bowl. Use your scraper to turn out the dough onto the work surface.

5 Form the dough into a ball following steps 20 to 23 on pages 50 to 52, and leave to rest in the bowl, covered, for about 1 hour, until just under double in size (see page 27).

6 Place a 12-inch baking ring on a baking sheet, then press in a large sheet of parchment paper. Beat the eggs with the salt in a small bowl to make the glaze.

7 Lightly flour your work surface again. Roll out the dough into a circle roughly the size of the baking ring.

MAKES 1 LARGE TART (12 INCHES IN DIAMETER), ENOUGH FOR ABOUT 12 SERVINGS

200g whole milk
2 large eggs
500g strong white bread flour, plus extra for dusting
20g compressed fresh yeast
60g superfine sugar
10g fine sea salt
50g cold unsalted butter
12 firm ripe plums, stoned and quartered
1 heaped tablespoon flaked almonds

For the almond cream:
75g unsalted butter, softened
75g superfine sugar
75g ground almonds
15g all-purpose flour
1 egg
1 tablespoon vanilla vodka (or rum or other spirit)

For the *crème pâtissière*:
3 egg yolks
60g superfine sugar
25g all-purpose flour
250g whole milk
1 vanilla pod

For the glaze:
2 eggs
pinch of fine sea salt
1 tablespoon whole milk

To serve:
confectioners' sugar, for dusting (optional)

8 Lower the dough into the lined baking ring, and with your fingertips, gently press it down in the center, and outwards into the shape of the ring, so that you create an indent big enough to take the plums, and form a rim around the outside.

9 Mix together the *crème pâtissière* and almond cream, and spoon evenly over the dough.

10 Cover the surface with the quartered plums, and scatter the slivered almonds over the top (see overleaf).

11 Leave to rise for about 45 minutes, and preheat the oven to 375°F.

12 Brush the rim of the dough with the egg glaze, put the baking sheet into the preheated oven, and turn the temperature down to 350°F. Bake for 10 minutes, then turn the heat down to 325°F and bake for about 25 minutes, until the rim of the tart is quite dark, and the cream is set. Leave to cool to room temperature, and dust with confectioners' sugar before serving, if you wish.

Petits pains with Gruyère

In France these little rolls are often sold in bakeries for making sandwiches (see overleaf). They also freeze well if you are not using them immediately.

MAKES 10 ROLLS

150g whole milk
150g cool water
1 extra-large egg
40g honey
50g extra virgin olive oil
500g strong white bread flour,
  plus extra for dusting
20g compressed fresh yeast
10g fine sea salt
50g cold unsalted butter
about 100g Gruyère (or
  Emmental or Cheddar)
  cheese, grated

For the glaze:
2 eggs
pinch of fine sea salt

1 Put the milk, water, egg, honey, and olive oil into the bowl of a food mixer, then add the flour. Break up the compressed fresh yeast, and add to one side of the bowl. Place the salt on the other side of the bowl to the yeast. Break the butter into pieces on top.

2 Mix on slow speed for 4 minutes, then turn the speed up to medium for about 10 to 12 minutes, until the dough comes away cleanly from the sides of the bowl.

3 Lightly flour the work surface, and also a clean bowl. Use your scraper to turn out the dough onto the work surface. Form the dough into a ball following steps 20 to 23 on pages 50 to 52, and leave to rest in the bowl, covered, for about 45 minutes, until just under double in size (see page 27).

4 Have ready two nonstick baking sheets, or line two baking sheets with parchment paper.

5 Divide the dough into 10 pieces of about 85g each, and then shape into small, chubbier versions of the Rustic Baguettes on pages 61 to 67, by following steps 17 to 25. Place the rolls on the prepared baking sheets. Cover with a baking cloth or a large freezer bag, and allow to rise for about 45 minutes to1 hour, until just under double in size.

6 While the rolls are rising, beat the eggs with the salt to make the glaze.

7 Preheat the oven to 375°F. Once the rolls have risen, brush the top of the rolls with the egg glaze.

8 Either use the tip of a sharp serrated-edged knife to make a deep slash lengthwise in the top of each roll, or make a series of snips with scissors, and push in a little of the grated cheese.

9 Transfer the baking sheets to the preheated oven, turn the heat down to 350°F, and bake for about 15 minutes, until the rolls are golden, and the cheese has colored a little. Allow to cool completely on a wire rack before eating.

English muffins

Ever since I first came to the UK, I have loved muffins, especially for breakfast, filled with ham or bacon and a soft fried or poached egg with its yolk running into the crumb: so good! You will need individual tart pans (about 4¾ inch diameter) to make these, or if you don't have enough pans, you can bake the muffins in batches—in which case leave half of the balls of dough, covered, in the fridge until ready to use.

MAKES 12 MUFFINS

1 quantity of *Pain de mie* dough (see page 139)
a little semolina flour, for dusting

1 Follow the *Pain de mie* method (see page 137) up to the end of step 3.

2 Divide into 12 pieces of just under 80g each (see step 15 on page 64) and shape into balls as before.

3 Put some semolina flour in a wide shallow bowl, and sprinkle a little into the base of each tart tin.

4 Flatten each ball of dough slightly with your hand, and press gently into the bowl of semolina, so each one is dusted well all over. Put into the pans, and cover with one or more large freezer bags. Leave to rise for 45 minutes, until the dough expands into the pans (see page 27).

5 Preheat the oven to 400°F. Have ready a baking sheet on which to pack the pans together as closely as possible.

6 Put the pans on the baking sheet, cover with a large sheet of parchment paper, and place one or two baking sheets on top of the parchment to keep the muffins flat.

7 Transfer to the hot oven and bake for 15 minutes, then remove the sheet or sheets used as weights and parchment, and bake for an additional 3 to 5 minutes. The muffins should be very light golden on top, but still quite pale around the sides. Turn the muffins onto a wire rack to cool completely.

Pain de mie

This recipe is a little richer than that in my first book, *Dough*, but still a simple, everyday bread. *Mie* is the French word for crumb, so this bread really is all about the inside, which should be much tighter than a lot of traditional French breads, and soft, thanks to the addition of a small quantity of butter and sugar. Also, there should be very little crust. It is always a big favorite with kids for sandwiches, and perfect for making Croque Monsieurs (see page 211), or *biscotte*. For this, the *pain de mie* is sliced and put into the oven to dry out at about 175 to 195°F. Then the heat is turned up to 400°F to color and crisp the slices quickly. *Biscottes* are eaten with butter and jam for breakfast. For fun, you could bake mini *pain de mie* in 95g pans. This recipe will make ten (you can keep the dough in the fridge, and shape and bake the loaves in batches (they will only need about 15 minutes in the oven).

MAKES 2 MEDIUM PAN LOAVES

150g whole milk
200g cool water
500g strong white bread flour, plus extra for dusting
10g compressed fresh yeast
20g superfine sugar
20g fine sea salt
50g cold unsalted butter
a little vegetable oil or butter, for greasing

---

1 Put the milk and water into the bowl of a food mixer, then add the flour. Break up the compressed fresh yeast, and add to one side of the bowl. Add the sugar and salt on the other side of the bowl to the yeast. Break up the butter on top. Mix on slow speed for 4 minutes, then increase the speed to medium for about 10 to 12 minutes, until the dough comes cleanly away from the sides of the bowl.

2 Lightly flour the work surface, and also a clean bowl. Use your scraper to turn out the dough onto the work surface.

3 Form the dough into a ball following steps 20 to 23 on pages 50 to 52, and leave to rest in a bowl, covered, for about 1½ hours, until just under double in size (see page 27).

4 Divide the dough in half (see step 15 on page 64); shape into balls, as above.

5 Lightly grease two medium bread pans with oil or butter, and place on a baking sheet. Gently press a ball of dough into each pan. Cover as before, and allow to rise until the dough has reached the top of the pans.

6 Preheat the oven to 450°F. Fill a clean spray bottle with water. Put the baking sheet into the preheated oven, and quickly mist the inside with a water spray just before closing the door. Although this bread has virtually no crust, the steam will help the crumb to develop. Bake for 20 to 25 minutes until golden brown, then remove from the tins and cool.

Leopard bread

So-called "tiger bread" has become so fashionable that people are always asking for it in the bakery. I prefer to call it "leopard bread", because the mottled markings that come from brushing the top of the loaf with a yeasty paste, which cracks and crisps in the oven, remind me more of the coat of a leopard than a tiger. However, the pattern on each loaf will turn out differently—which is the fun of it—so sometimes "crocodile bread" might be more appropriate! Again, the dough I use is the same as for the *Pain de mie*.

Many commercial tiger breads are made with ready-to-use pastes containing artificial flavorings, but you will taste a big difference when you make your own from scratch. I like to use beer in the paste, which increases its yeasty character, but you need such a small quantity, that unless you plan to drink the rest of the bottle, you can use water if you prefer. Incidentally, you can use this paste to decorate other breads in exactly the same way.

MAKES 1 OVAL LOAF

1 quantity dough ingredients for *Pain de mie* (see page 137)

For the paste:
100g rice flour, plus extra for dusting
5g compressed fresh yeast
10g superfine sugar
10g sesame oil
50g beer or water

1 Follow the *Pain de mie* method on page 137 up to the end of step 3, then gently elongate the ball of dough into an oval shape, and place on a baking sheet to rise for 1 hour (see page 27).

2 While the dough is rising, make the paste by mixing the rice flour with the rest of the ingredients in a bowl. It will thicken slightly by the time the dough has finished rising.

3 Brush the top and sides of the dough with a thick layer of the paste, then dust the extra rice flour generously over the top, using a small strainer.

4 Leave for 1 to 1¼ hours in a cool place until the paste has cracked all over (see page 138).

5 Preheat the oven to 425°F. Fill a clean spray bottle with water.

6 Transfer the baking sheet to the preheated oven, and just before closing the door, quickly mist the oven, avoiding spraying the bread itself too much.

7 After 10 minutes, turn the oven down to between 425°F and 400°F and bake for an additional 15 minutes, then turn it down again to 400°F for a final 10 minutes. Open the oven, so that it is slightly ajar for the last 2 to 3 minutes to achieve a really good crust. The bread should be dark golden, and patterned like a leopard, tiger, or crocodile (see page 139)! Turn onto a wire rack to cool completely.

Chocolate, pistachio, and orange loaf

There is something magical about the combination of chocolate chips, bright green pistachios, and oranges that makes this a huge favorite in our bakery. However, you can play around with the chocolate, nuts, and citrus fruits as you like, perhaps substituting white chocolate, hazelnuts, and lemon zest.

MAKES 10 SMALL LOAVES

150g good-quality dark
  chocolate chips
75g crushed pistachios
zest of 2 oranges
50g candied peel
1 tablespoon Cointreau
  (optional)
125g unsalted butter
125g whole milk
3 extra-large eggs
500g strong white bread flour,
  plus extra for dusting
15g compressed fresh yeast
45g superfine sugar
10g fine sea salt

For the glaze:
2 eggs
pinch of fine sea salt

1 Mix together the chocolate chips, pistachios, orange zest, and candied peel in a bowl. Stir in the Cointreau (if using), and set aside.

2 To make the dough, place the cold butter between two sheets of waxed paper, and bash it with the end of a rolling pin to soften and break it up into small pieces.

3 Put the milk and eggs into the bowl of a food mixer, then add the flour. Break up the compressed fresh yeast, and add to one side of the bowl. Add the sugar and salt on the other side of the bowl to the yeast. Mix on slow speed for 4 minutes.

4 Increase the speed to medium, and after 2 minutes, add the softened butter, piece by piece, until it is all incorporated. Continue on medium speed for about 10 to 12 minutes, until the dough comes away cleanly from the sides of the bowl.

5 Add the chocolate and pistachio mixture, and mix for no longer than 30 to 40 seconds on the lowest speed—don't let the chocolate chips and nuts become mushy.

6 Lightly flour the work surface, and also a clean bowl. Use a scraper to turn out the dough onto the work surface.

7 Form the dough into a ball following steps 20 to 23 on pages 50 to 52, and leave to rest in the bowl, covered, for about 45 minutes, until just under double in size (see page 27).

8 Lightly flour the work surface again, and divide the dough into 10 pieces, each weighing about 110g.

There is something magical about the combination of chocolate chips, bright green pistachios, and oranges that makes this a huge favorite in our bakery.

9 Re-form the dough into balls as before and press gently into lined wooden baking boxes or pans. Cover as before, and leave to rise for about 1 hour, until just under double in size.

10 While the dough is rising, preheat the oven to 375°F, and beat the eggs in a small bowl with the salt for the glaze.

11 Brush the top of each loaf with the egg glaze, and use scissors to snip into the dough for decoration.

12 Place the pans or boxes on a baking sheet, and put into the preheated oven, turn the heat down to 350°F, and bake for 15 to 20 minutes until golden.

Kouign amann

This is a traditional bread-cake, made with a buttery, caramelized dough from my native Brittany. It contains a lot of butter ("amann" is the Breton word for butter) which is layered into the dough. When I was growing up, this was a real treat, one that our family often had after Sunday lunch. It is said that *Kouign amann* was first made in 1860 in the town of Douarnenez, on the coast of Finistère, when a boulangerie ran out of cake, and the baker was told to create something quickly. As he was not a pâtissier, used to making intricate confections, he stuck to the skills he knew, and rolled out some bread dough, scattered it with pieces of butter, sprinkled it with sugar, then folded it several times, and shaped it as if making bread. The result is something between a cake and a caramelized loaf, and it has become the specialty of the town. All over Brittany, people have since developed their own recipes and methods. At the local bakery where I was an apprentice, my boss made one of the best versions I ever tasted. Although he kept his recipe a close secret, I watched him make it many times, so the way I make my *Kouign amann* is based on his technique. A generous slice of it, cut while still warm, is beautiful with a bowl of good hard cider.

You can use a mixer, but I prefer to make the dough for this by hand. The longer you rest the dough in the fridge, the more its flavor develops—keep it overnight if you can, then let it rise before baking the next day.

MAKES ONE LARGE TART (12 INCHES IN DIAMETER), ENOUGH FOR 10 TO 12 SERVINGS

500g strong white bread flour, plus extra for dusting
10g compressed fresh yeast
10g fine sea salt
260g superfine sugar
350g water
200g salted butter
2 tablespoons whole milk, for glazing

---

1 Put the flour in a large mixing bowl. Break up the compressed fresh yeast on one side of the bowl, and have the salt on the other. Lightly rub the yeast into the flour between the flats of your hands, as if you were washing your hands. Stir in 10g of the sugar.

2 Add the water, and follow steps 5 to 23 on pages 39 to 52.

3 Leave to rest for at least 1 hour, then put the bowl in the fridge, covered as before, for a minimum of 4 hours, or preferably overnight.

4 When ready to bake, preheat the oven to 375°F.

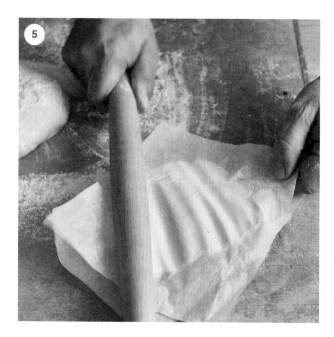

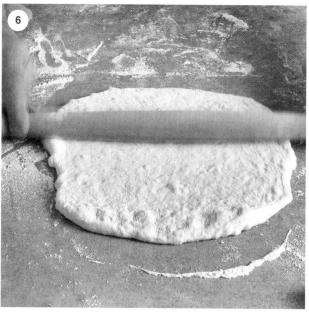

5 Take the butter from the fridge, and place it between two sheets of waxed paper, then bash it with a rolling pin into a square shape. It should be really soft, but still cold.

6 Lightly flour the work surface, and turn out the dough so that the top side is underneath. Dust the surface lightly with flour. Roll it into a rough rectangle about the size of a letter. Bash the butter again until it is about ¼ inch thick, and roughly the same size and shape as the dough.

7 With the longer side of the dough facing you, peel the top sheet of waxed paper from the butter, and use the sheet underneath to lift up the butter, and flip it on top of the dough. Peel off the second sheet of paper.

8 Use your fingertips to gently push the butter into the dough.

9 Sprinkle 200g of the sugar over the butter, and again with your fingertips, gently push the sugar into the butter.

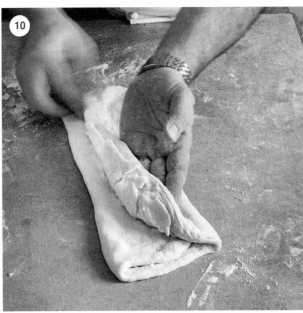

10 Fold one short end of the dough into the center, then fold the other short end over the top to create three layers.

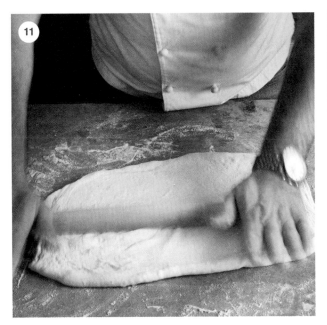

11 Lightly flour the work surface again, and roll the dough very gently into a rough rectangle a little longer than before.

12 Turn the dough so that the short side is facing you. Fold one end into the center.

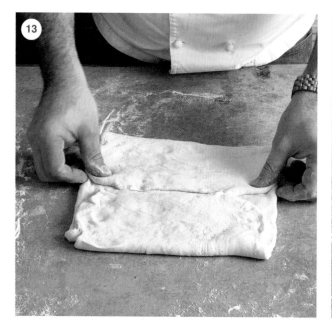

13 Fold the other end into the center, so that the edges are just touching in the middle.

14 Now fold one side over the other to create four layers.

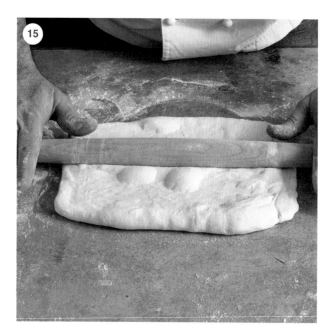

15 Lightly roll the dough until it is a rough square that will fit into your baking ring.

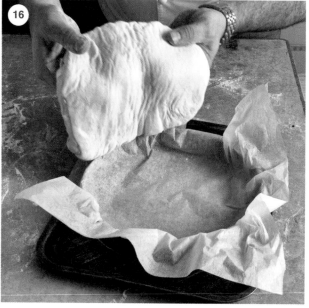

16 Place a baking ring (about 12 inches in diameter and 2½ inches deep) on top of a baking sheet, then press in a large sheet of parchment paper. Turn the dough over, and onto the parchment, and using your fingertips, gently push it outward so that it fits the shape of the ring.

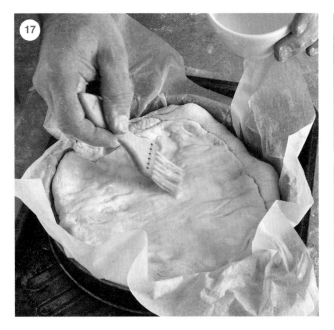

17 Brush off any excess flour from the surface of the dough, and then brush all over with the milk.

18 Sprinkle with the remaining sugar.

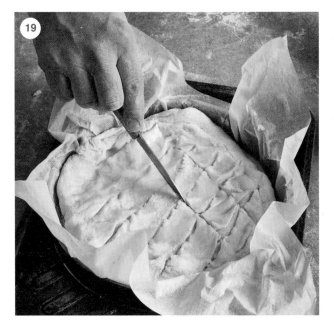

19 Use a sharp knife to score the surface of the dough in criss-cross fashion. This will prevent the dough from puffing up too much.

20 Bake in the preheated oven for 40 minutes, until the top and the base are really dark brown and well caramelized.

21 Remove from the oven and leave for about 10 minutes. Place a large plate over the top, and firmly holding the baking sheet underneath, quickly invert so that the *Kouign amann* ends up on the plate. Be very careful when you do this, because hot caramel will burn.

Toasted pine nut, honey, and pear croustades,

When pears are out of season, don't be ashamed to use canned ones for this recipe: French bakers use these all the time. You could also use fresh or canned peaches. The method for folding the dough is the same as the previous recipe.

MAKES 12 PASTRIES

200g whole milk
2 extra-large eggs
500g strong white bread flour,
  plus extra for dusting
30g compressed fresh yeast
50g superfine sugar
10g fine sea salt
200g cold unsalted butter

For the pears:
1 liter water
500g superfine sugar
6 small ripe fresh pears,
  pared, but left whole

For the pine nuts:
300g pine nuts
100g honey

For the glaze:
1 egg
2 tablespoons whole milk

1 First prepare the pears (unless you are using canned ones). Bring the water and sugar to a boil in a pan, then simmer until you have a light syrup. Put in the whole pears, and simmer gently for 20 minutes, then remove from the heat, lift out the pears and leave to cool. Reserve the syrup to glaze the croustades once they come out of the oven.

2 Put the milk and eggs into the bowl of a food mixer, then add the flour. Break up the compressed fresh yeast, and add to one side of the bowl. Add the sugar and salt on the other side of the bowl to the yeast. Mix on slow speed for 4 minutes, then increase the speed to medium and continue to mix for about 10 to 12 minutes, until the dough comes away cleanly from the sides of the bowl.

3 Lightly flour the work surface, and also a clean bowl. Use your scraper to turn out the dough onto the work surface.

4 Form the dough into a ball following steps 20 to 23 on pages 50 to 52, and leave to rest in the bowl, covered, for about 45 minutes, until just under double in size.

5 Take the butter from the fridge and follow steps 5 to 14 of the *Kouign amann* recipe on pages 146 to 148, omitting the sprinkling of sugar.

6 Lift the folded dough onto a plastic tray or a baking pan lined with parchment paper. Cover with a large freezer bag, and rest in the fridge for at least 15 minutes.

7 Now repeat steps 11 to 14 on pages 147 to 148 and rest for 15 minutes in the fridge as before or put in the fridge to rest overnight if you don't want to use the dough immediately.

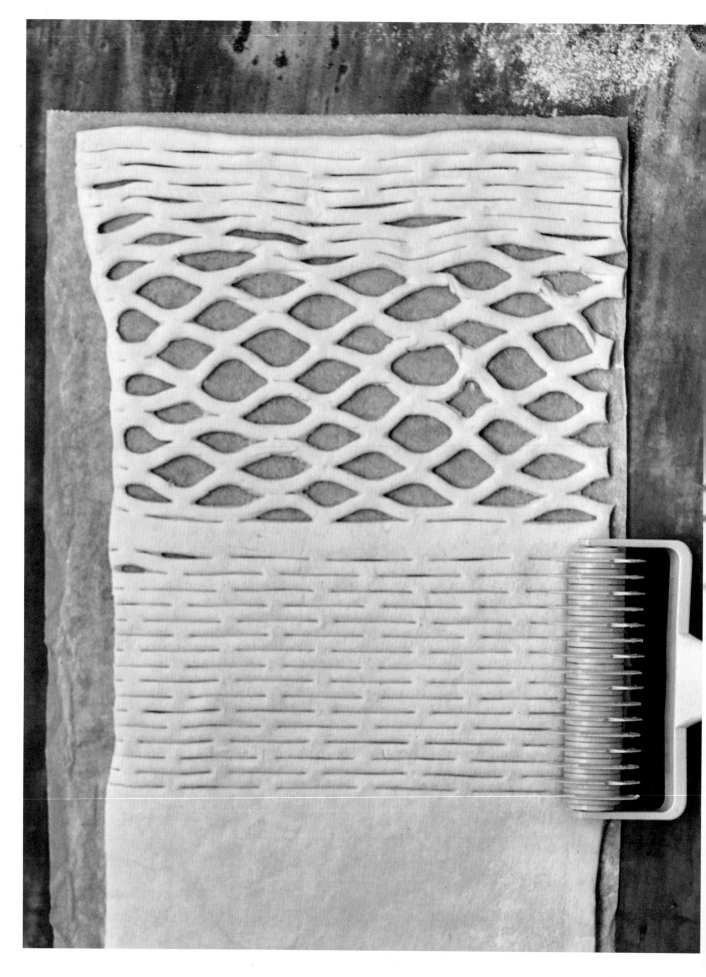

8 When ready to bake, put the pine nuts into a dry skillet, and toast them lightly until colored all over. Add the honey, and keep stirring until the nuts are caramelized—take care not to let the honey burn—then remove from the heat.

9 Take the pan of dough from the fridge. Lightly flour the work surface, and roll the dough into a rectangle approximately 11 x 16 inches. Cut in half, lengthwise, then cut one of the halves into 12 squares. Beat the eggs and milk in a small bowl for the glaze.

10 Lift out the cooled pears from the pan, reserving the syrup. Halve, then core each pear. Place the halves cut-side down, and make a series of cuts, leaving the pear joined at the stalk end, and then fan out. Place a fanned-out pear half on each square, and sprinkle with some of the caramelized nuts. Brush the edges of the dough with a little of the glaze.

11 Take a lattice cutter and roll it over the other half of the dough, then cut the dough into 12 squares. Place a lattice square over the top of each pear and nuts square, opening out the lattice slightly as you do so. Then press around all the edges to seal.

12 Transfer the squares to a baking sheet, lined with parchment paper, cover with a large freezer bag, and leave to rise for 45 minutes to 1 hour, until the dough is just under double in size. Preheat the oven to 375°F.

13 Brush the rest of the egg and milk glaze over the tops of the *croustades*, put the pan into the preheated oven, and turn down the heat to 350°F. Bake for 20 to 25 minutes, until the lattice-work and the base of the squares are golden. While still warm, brush with the reserved syrup from poaching the pears.

Almond and cherry slices and rolls

You can either bake these as open slices, in which case the dough will puff up around the almond paste and cherries, or encase the fruit and paste in the dough to resemble sweet versions of sausage rolls. If you are making rolls, then halve the cherries and remove the pits. For the open slices I like to leave the cherries whole—but if you do this, remember to warn people!

1 Follow steps 2 to 7 on page 150 to make the dough.

2 While the dough is resting, put all the ingredients for the paste in a bowl, and use a wooden spoon to mix together thoroughly.

3 Take the tray of dough from the fridge. Lightly flour the work surface, and roll the dough into a rectangle approximately 11 x 16 inches. Cut it into 12 squares.

4 Beat the eggs with the salt in a small bowl for the glaze.

5 Spoon or pipe a strip of the paste down the center of each square and then put a row of cherries on top. (If you prefer to make rolls, brush the edges of the dough with a little of the egg glaze, then fold the dough over the top of the cherries as if making a sausage roll and press down to seal).

6 Transfer to a baking sheet, cover with a large freezer bag, and allow to rise for 45 minutes to 1 hour, until just under double in size (see page 27). If you have opted for open slices, the dough will form a rim around the paste and cherries. While the dough rises, preheat the oven to 375°F.

7 Brush the edges of the slices (or the tops of the rolls) with the rest of the egg glaze. Put the baking sheet into the preheated oven, and turn down the heat to 350°F. Bake for 20 to 25 minutes, until the tops are golden.

8 Meanwhile, make the rum glaze. Put the sugar, rum, and water in a pan, and bring to a boil, then simmer until you have a light syrup. Brush over the slices (or rolls) while still hot, then allow to cool.

MAKES 12 SLICES OR ROLLS

200g whole milk
2 extra-large eggs
500g strong white bread flour,
   plus extra for dusting
30g compressed fresh yeast
50g superfine sugar
10g fine sea salt
200g cold unsalted butter
500g fresh cherries (see note
   above)

For the paste:
150g ground almonds
150g fine bread crumbs
150g superfine sugar
1 heaping teaspoon ground
   cinnamon
½ teaspoon ground cardamom
2 eggs
150g whole milk
zest of 1 lemon
1 capful of dark rum

For the egg glaze:
2 eggs
pinch of fine sea salt

For the rum glaze:
100g superfine sugar
2 tablespoons dark rum
100g water

Cinnamon knots

I first saw these on one of my many trips to Denmark, where they are sold in every bakery. In my baking classes, everyone loves the rich combination of cinnamon, brown sugar, and butter.

1 Follow steps 2 to 7 on page 150 to make the dough.

2 Take the pan of dough from the fridge. Lightly flour the work surface and roll the dough into a rectangle approximately 11 x 16 inches.

3 For the filling, beat the butter and sugar together until pale, and stir in the cinnamon. Spread the mixture over the top of the dough.

4 With the long side facing you, fold the dough in half lengthwise to enclose the filling, and slice it widthwise into 12 strips each roughly 1½ inches across. Then, using a sharp knife, cut twice down the length of each strip to make three strands, see overleaf. Braid the three strands together, and repeat to make 12 individual braids.

5 Take each braid, and roll it up along its length to create a knot (see the picture overleaf). Lay the knots on a baking sheet lined with parchment paper, cover with a large freezer bag, and allow to rise for 1 hour (see page 27).

6 While the knots are rising, preheat the oven to 375°F, and beat the eggs with the milk in a small bowl for the egg glaze.

7 Brush the knots with the egg glaze, put the baking sheet into the preheated oven, and turn down the heat to 350°F. Bake for about 18 to 20 minutes, until golden.

8 Meanwhile, make the sugar glaze. Put the sugar and water in a pan, and bring to a boil, then simmer until you have a light syrup. Brush over the knots while still hot, then allow to cool.

MAKES 12 KNOTS

200g whole milk
2 large eggs
600g strong white bread flour
25g compressed fresh yeast
50g superfine sugar
10g fine sea salt
200g cold unsalted butter

For the filling:
150g unsalted butter
250g soft brown sugar
2 teaspoons cinnamon

For the egg glaze:
1 egg
2 tablespoons whole milk

For the sugar glaze:
100g superfine sugar
100g water

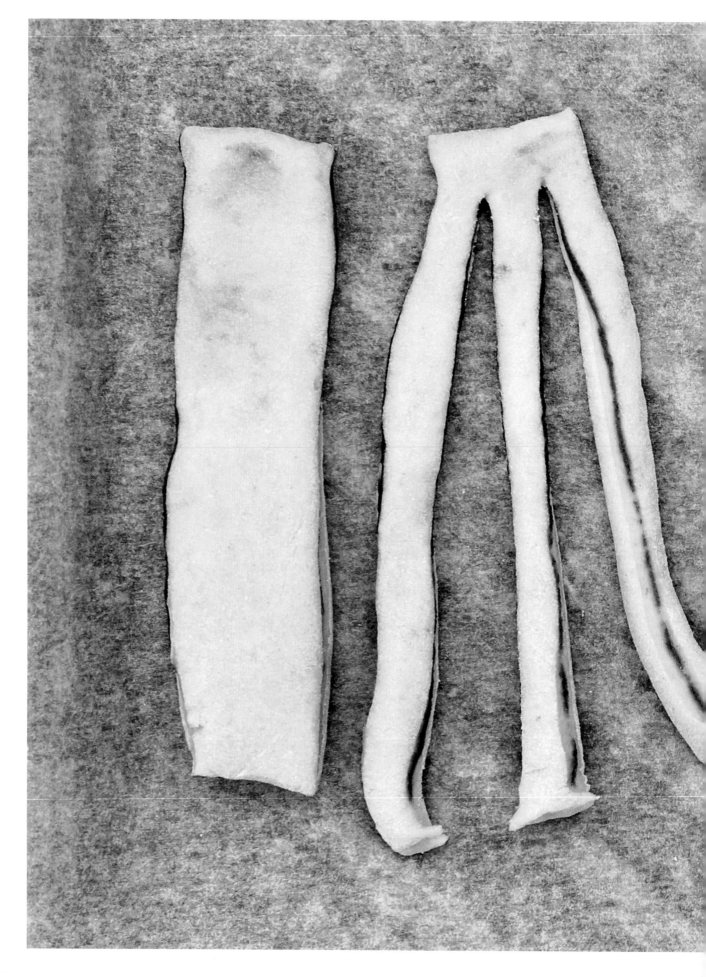

Cheese twists

This is the dough that bakers know as *pâte feuilletée*, which is used for Danish pastries and "viennoiserie." It is also used in the recipes for Toasted pine nut, honey, and pear croustades on page 150, Almond and cherry slices on page 155 and the folding technique is the same as for *Kouign amann* on page 145. If you allow the dough to rest overnight in the fridge, you will achieve a more flaky, open crumb.

1 Put the milk and eggs into the bowl of a food mixer, then add the flour. Break up the compressed fresh yeast and add to one side of the bowl. Add the sugar, and place the salt on the other side of the bowl to the yeast.

2 Mix on slow speed for 4 minutes, then increase the speed to medium, and continue to mix for about 12 to 14 minutes, until the dough comes away cleanly from the sides of the bowl.

3 Lightly flour the work surface, and also a clean bowl. Use your scraper to turn out the dough onto the work surface.

4 Form the dough into a ball following steps 20 to 23 on pages 50 to 52, and leave to rest in the bowl, covered, for about 45 minutes, until just under double in size (see page 27).

5 Take the butter from the fridge and follow steps 5 to 14 of the *Kouign amann* recipe on pages 146 to 148.

6 Lift the folded dough onto a plastic tray or a baking sheet lined with parchment paper. Cover with a freezer bag, and rest in the fridge for at least 15 minutes.

7 Now repeat steps 11 to 14. Rest again for 15 minutes in the fridge as before, or put in the fridge to rest overnight if you don't want to use the dough immediately.

8 Take the pan from the fridge and lightly roll the dough into a rectangle approximately 11 x 16 inches.

MAKES 12–14 CHUNKY TWISTS

200g whole milk
2 large eggs
500g strong white bread flour, plus extra for dusting
30g compressed fresh yeast
50g superfine sugar
10g fine sea salt
200g cold unsalted butter

For the flavoring:
about 100g good strong cheese, such as Cheddar, grated
a little paprika, preferably smoked

If you leave the dough
to rest overnight in the
fridge, you will achieve
a more flaky, open crumb.

9 Preheat the oven to 190°C and have ready two non-stick baking sheets, or line two baking sheets with parchment paper.

10 Sprinkle the grated cheese over the top of the dough, pressing the cheese into the dough quite firmly with your fingertips. Dust with the paprika.

11 Fold in half lengthwise, so that the cheese is enclosed inside, then cut lengthwise into strips about ¾ to 1¼ inch wide, and twist each length.

12 Lay the twists on the prepared pans, cover with a baking cloth or a large freezer bag, and leave to rise for 30 minutes.

13 Transfer the pans to the preheated oven, turn down the heat to 350°F, and bake for about 12 to 15 minutes, until light golden brown. Cool on a wire rack before eating.

Salted caramel brioches

Salted caramels were created in my hometown of Quiberon in Brittany, by a chocolatier named Henri le Roux using the local butter studded with sea salt crystals. To me they are the best chocolates in the world—my mom sends me a box every Christmas. I use salted Breton butter in this recipe, but there are also very good equivalents made by dairies in the UK.

The salted caramel can be stored in a clean jar in the fridge for up to a month, and it's great for topping *tartines* (see page 212), so it is worth making a larger quantity.

(see page 212)

MAKES ABOUT 4

125g whole milk
4 extra-large eggs
500g strong white bread
   flour
15g compressed fresh yeast
45g superfine sugar
10g fine sea salt
60g cold unsalted butter

For the salted caramel:
100g blanched hazelnuts, plus
   extra to decorate
250g water
450g superfine sugar
200g butter made with sea salt
   crystals (or unsalted butter
   plus a heaping teaspoon of
   sea salt flakes)
200g heavy cream or crème
   fraîche
1 teaspoon good cocoa
   powder

For the glaze:
2 eggs
pinch of fine sea salt

1 First make the caramel. Toast the hazelnuts in a dry skillet until golden all over, but take care not to let them burn. Allow to cool, then either finely chop, or pulse briefly in a blender; you want small pieces of nut, not a powder.

2 Pour the water into a pan, bring to a simmer, then add the sugar slowly. Allow to dissolve and bring to a boil. Watch it carefully, and take off the heat as soon as it turns an amber caramel color.

3 Stir in the butter, and as soon as it is incorporated, stir in the cream and the cocoa powder. Finally stir in the chopped nuts, and leave to cool.

4 To make the dough, put the milk and eggs into the bowl of a food mixer, then add the flour. Break up the compressed fresh yeast and add to one side of the bowl. Add the sugar and salt on the other side of the bowl to the yeast. Break up the butter into pieces on top. Mix on slow speed for 4 minutes, then increase to medium for about 10 to 12 minutes, until you have a dough that comes cleanly away from the sides of the bowl.

5 Lightly flour the work surface, and a clean bowl. Use a scraper to turn out the dough onto the work surface.

6 Form the dough into a ball following steps 20 to 23 on pages 50 to 52, and leave to rest in the bowl for about 45 minutes, until just under double in size.

7 Lightly flour a work surface again, and use your fingertips to press out the dough into a rectangle roughly 11 x 16 inches. Cut the dough into four equal pieces.

8 Spoon three or four nuggets of the cooled caramel on top of each piece of dough—not too many, otherwise the caramel will ooze out of the dough when it is in the oven and burn. Reserve the rest of the caramel.

Salted caramels were created in my hometown of Quiberon in Brittany, by a chocolatier named Henri le Roux using the local butter studded with sea salt crystals.

9 Gather up the dough as if forming into a ball (as before), so that you completely enclose the caramel.

10 Turn the balls over so that they are smooth-side up, and place them on a baking sheet lined with parchment paper. Cover with a baking cloth or a large freezer bag and allow to rise for 1 hour.

11 While the dough is rising, beat the eggs with the salt in a small bowl for the glaze.

12 Preheat the oven to 375°F.

13 Brush the tops of the buns with the egg glaze, then use scissors to make a series of snips in the top of each. Sprinkle with the extra hazelnuts.

14 Put the baking sheet into the preheated oven, turn down the heat to 350°F, and bake for about 15 to 20 minutes, until dark golden brown.

15 Remove from the oven, and while the buns are still hot, spoon some more nuggets of caramel on top, which will melt into the bread.

Caramelized apple and calvados brioche

This is not the simplest to put together, but it is a real showstopper of a Sunday dessert: half cake, half dessert: gooey and beautiful, with some extra crème fraîche on the side. Make sure you slice the apple for the top really thinly—preferably using a mandoline—so the slices look like crispy leaves.

---

1 First prepare the caramelized apples. Chop the prepared apples into rough dice (about ½ inch).

2 Heat the butter in a skillet until it begins to turn brown, then add the apple, and toss well to coat. Add the sugar, and cook, moving the pieces around, until they take on a little color.

3 Pour in the calvados, and carefully light it using a match. When the flame has died down, add the crème fraîche, and allow to simmer for a couple of minutes. Remove from the heat, and leave to cool.

4 To make the dough, put the milk and eggs into the bowl of a food mixer, then add the flour. Break up the compressed fresh yeast and add to one side of the bowl. Add the sugar and salt on the other side of the bowl to the yeast. Break up the butter on top. Mix on slow speed for 4 minutes, then turn up the speed to medium for about 10 to 12 minutes, until the dough comes cleanly away from the sides of the bowl.

5 Lightly flour the work surface, and also a clean bowl. Use your scraper to turn out the dough onto the work surface.

6 Form the dough into a ball following steps 20 to 23 on pages 50 to 52, and leave to rest in the bowl, covered, for about 1 hour, until just under double in size (see page 27).

7 Grease an 8½-inch diameter cake pan with butter.

8 Lightly flour your work surface again, and turn out the dough. Press and prod it into a rectangle about 11 x 16 inches.

MAKES 1 LARGE LOAF (8½ INCHES IN DIAMETER)

250g whole milk
2 extra-large eggs
500g strong white bread flour, plus extra for dusting
30g compressed fresh yeast
80g superfine sugar
10g fine sea salt
80g cold unsalted butter, plus extra for greasing the pan

For the caramelized apples:
4 eating apples, pared and cored
40g unsalted butter
100g superfine sugar
1 small glass of calvados (about 70g)
50g crème fraîche

For the glaze:
2 eggs
pinch of fine sea salt

To decorate:
1 eating apple, pared, cored, and sliced very thinly
about 1 tablespoon pearl sugar
confectioners' sugar, for dusting (optional)

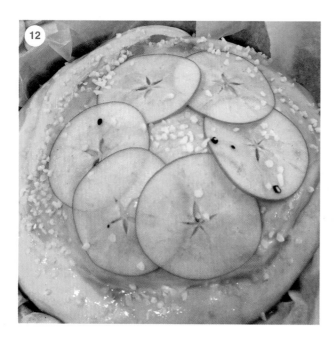

9 Spread the caramelized apple evenly over the dough and roll up lengthwise —not too tightly—to form a long log, then coil this into the pan.

10 Cover with a baking cloth or large freezer bag, and allow to rise for at least an hour, until the dough comes to just above the rim of the pan.

11 While the brioche is rising, preheat the oven to 375°F, and beat the eggs with the salt in a small bowl for the glaze.

12 Brush the top of the coiled brioche with the egg glaze, and decorate with the slices of apple, then sprinkle over the pearl sugar.

13 Bake in the preheated oven for about 10 minutes, then turn down to 350°F for an additional 35 to 40 minutes, until the brioche pulls away slightly from the edges of the pan and a skewer inserted into the middle comes out hot and clean. To color the top a little more, turn down the heat to 300°F for a few more minutes.

14 Leave to stand for about 10 to 15 minutes, then turn out of the pan, and cool on a wire rack. If you wish, dust with some confectioners' sugar before serving.

Rum and golden raisin brioches

I am a big fan of rum for soaking fruit, as it really brings out the rich, sweet flavors, which marry so well with the brioche. In our bread classes, I always serve prunes in rum from a big jar with coffee at break time—and they always put a smile on people's faces.

1 Start by making the ferment. Put 100g of the flour in a bowl, and break up 10g of the yeast on top. Mix in the milk, and leave at room temperature for at least 6 hours, but preferably overnight.

2 In a separate bowl, mix the golden raisins and rum, and leave to macerate, again at room temperature, and preferably overnight.

3 To make the dough, transfer the ferment to the bowl of a food mixer, add the eggs and cream, then add the rest of the flour and yeast. Add the sugar and salt on the other side of the bowl to the yeast. Break up the butter on top. Mix on slow speed for 4 minutes, then increase the speed to medium for about 10 to 12 minutes, until the dough comes cleanly away from the sides of the bowl.

4 Drain the macerated golden raisins (if there is any rum remaining, you can add it to the syrup for the glaze) and add the fruit to the dough. Mix for no longer than 30 to 40 seconds on the lowest speed—you don't want the raisins to become mushy.

5 Lightly flour the work surface, and also a clean bowl. Use your scraper to turn out the dough onto the work surface.

6 Form the dough into a tight ball following steps 20 to 23 on pages 50 to 52, and leave to rest in the bowl, covered, for about 45 minutes, until just under double in size (see page 27).

7 Grease a 12-hole muffin pan. Lightly flour the work surface again, and divide the dough into 12 pieces weighing about 100g each (see step 15 on page 64).

MAKES 12 MUFFIN-SIZED BRIOCHES

500g strong white bread flour, plus extra for dusting
30g compressed fresh yeast
100g whole milk, at room temperature
2 tablespoons dark rum
250g golden raisins
3 extra-large eggs
100g heavy cream
60g sugar
10g fine sea salt
80g cold butter, plus a little extra for greasing

For the glaze:
2 eggs
pinch of fine sea salt

For the rum glaze:
100g superfine sugar
2 tablespoons dark rum
100g water

To decorate:
about 2 tablespoons slivered almonds

I am a big fan of rum for soaking fruit, as it really brings out the rich, sweet flavors which marry so well with the brioche.

8 Form each piece into a ball as before. Place, seam-side down, into the holes of the prepared pan, cover with a baking cloth or a large freezer bag, and leave to rise for 1 to 1¼ hours, until just under double in size.

9 While the brioches are rising, preheat the oven to 375°F, and beat the eggs with the salt in a small bowl for the glaze.

10 Brush the brioche tops with the egg glaze, and use scissors to snip a cross into the top of each one. Sprinkle with the slivered almonds to decorate.

11 Transfer the pan to the preheated oven, turn down the heat to 350°F, and bake for about 15 to 20 minutes until dark golden.

12 To make the rum glaze, put the sugar, rum (including any left over from soaking the fruit), and water in a pan, and bring to a boil, then turn down to a simmer until you have a thick syrup.

13 Remove the pan from the oven, turn out the brioches onto a wire rack, and while still warm, brush the tops with the rum glaze.

Challah

This is a Jewish speciality traditionally made on Sundays and holidays. The dough is normally made with oil, but I like to add a little butter, which brings the crumb a little closer to brioche. The strands of dough can be formed into a simple braid, or for important occasions, specialist bakeries might make large celebratory breads with up to eight or ten braids. I like to make a "double decker" with one braid on top of another, as in this recipe.

MAKES 1 BRAIDED LOAF

250g whole milk
1 medium egg
60g honey
50g extra virgin olive oil
500g strong white bread flour,
  plus extra for dusting
20g compressed fresh yeast
10g fine sea salt
50g cold unsalted butter

For the glaze:
2 eggs
pinch of fine sea salt

To decorate:
100g sesame seeds or poppy
  seeds (optional)

1 Put the milk, egg, honey, and olive oil into the bowl of a food mixer, then add the flour. Break up the compressed fresh yeast, and add to one side of the bowl. Add the salt on the other side of the bowl to the yeast. Break up the butter on top. Mix on slow speed for 4 minutes, then increase the speed to medium, and continue to mix for about 10 to 12 minutes, until the dough comes cleanly away from the sides of the bowl.

2 Lightly flour the work surface, and also a clean bowl. Use a scraper to turn out the dough onto the work surface.

3 Form the dough into a ball following steps 20 to 23 on pages 50 to 52, and leave to rest in the bowl, covered, for about 45 minutes, until just under double in size (see page 27).

4 Lightly flour the work surface again, turn out the dough and re-form into a ball as above. Leave to rest for an additional 45 minutes.

5 Re-flour the work surface lightly, and use your scraper to divide the dough into 7 pieces each weighing about 130g.

6 Following steps 17 to 24 on pages 64 to 66, roll each piece into a "rope" about ¾ inch in diameter.

7 To make the base, braid together 4 of the ropes, then press a rolling pin lightly along the length, in the center of the braid, enough to make an indentation (see overleaf).

8 Braid the remaining 3 ropes together, and lay this braid into the indentation you have made. Shape and press the 2 braids together at each end.

The strands of dough can be
braided into a simple braid,
or for important occasions,
specialist bakeries might make
large celebratory breads with
up to eight or ten braids.

9 Lift the challah onto a baking tray lined with parchment paper. Cover with a baking cloth or a large freezer bag and allow to rise for about 1 hour, until just under double in size.

10 While the challah is rising, beat the eggs with the salt in a small bowl for the glaze. Preheat the oven to 375°F.

11 Brush the top of the challah with the egg glaze and sprinkle with sesame seeds or poppy seeds (if using).

12 Transfer to the preheated oven, turn the heat down to 350°F and bake for about 35 to 40 minutes, until the challah is dark golden brown on top and underneath. Cool on a wire rack.

Russian braid

This is my version of the braided loaf, which in Russia is known as Babka. The loaves will keep for a few days wrapped in waxed paper—though I doubt you will be able to resist eating them immediately! You can rise and bake the dough in a tin if you prefer.

---

1 First make the chocolate *crème pâtissière*. Put the egg yolks and sugar into a bowl, and whisk until pale and creamy. Add the flour, and mix until smooth.

2 Pour the milk into a heavy-bottomed pan. Slice the vanilla bean along its length using a sharp knife. Open out and scrape the seeds into the milk, then put the halved bean in too.

3 Place the pan over medium heat, and bring the milk to just under a boil, then take off the heat. Slowly pour half of the hot flavored milk into the egg mixture, whisking well. Add the remainder of the milk, and whisk in well, then pour the mixture back into the pan.

4 Bring to a boil, continuing to whisk. Keep boiling and whisking continuously for 1 minute, then take off the heat, add the chocolate chips, and pour into a clean bowl.

5 Scoop out the vanilla bean halves, and cover the surface of the bowl with waxed paper immediately, as this will help to prevent a skin from forming as the custard cools. (You can wash and dry the vanilla beans, and use them to flavor either a jar of sugar, or a bottle of vodka—as in the next recipe.)

6 To make the dough, put the milk, egg, honey, and olive oil into the bowl of a food mixer, then add the flour. Break up the compressed fresh yeast and add to one side of the bowl. Add the salt on the other side of the bowl to the yeast. Break up the butter on top. Mix on slow speed for 4 minutes, then turn up the speed to medium for about 10 to 12 minutes, until the dough comes cleanly away from the sides of the bowl.

7 Lightly flour the work surface, and also a clean bowl. Use your scraper to turn out the dough onto the work surface.

8 Form the dough into a ball following steps 20 to 23 on pages 50 to 52, and leave to rest in the bowl, covered, for about 45 minutes, until just under double in size (see page 27).

MAKES 2 LOAVES

250g whole milk
1 large egg
60g honey
50g extra virgin olive oil
500g strong white bread flour, plus extra for dusting
30g compressed fresh yeast
10g fine sea salt
50g unsalted butter
handful of golden raisins (optional)

For the chocolate crème pâtissière:
3 egg yolks
60g superfine sugar
40g all-purpose flour
250g whole milk
1 vanilla bean
100g good-quality dark chocolate chips

For the glaze:
2 eggs
pinch of fine sea salt

For the rum glaze:
100g superfine sugar
2 tablespoons rum
100g water

9 Lightly flour the work surface again, turn out the dough, and re-form into a ball as before. Place back in the bowl, cover again, and rest for an additional 30 minutes.

10 Re-flour your work surface, and roll out the dough into a rectangle about 16 x 12 inches. Spread the cooled chocolate *crème pâtissière* over the top and add the sultanas, if using. Roll up the dough tightly lengthwise like a jelly roll, then cut in half crosswise, so that you have 2 rolls of equal size.

11 Cut the first roll in half lengthwise so that you expose the chocolate filling, and twist the 2 lengths together. Repeat with the second roll.

12 Place on a baking sheet lined with parchment paper, cover with a large freezer bag, and allow to rise for 45 minutes to 1 hour, until just under double in size.

13 While the loaves are rising, preheat the oven to 375°F, and beat the eggs with the salt in a small bowl for the glaze.

14 Glaze the top of each loaf with the egg glaze, transfer the baking sheet to the preheated oven, and turn the temperature down to 350°F. Bake for 20 to 25 minutes, until the *crème pâtissière* has set and the dough is shiny.

15 Meanwhile make the rum glaze. Put the sugar, rum, and water in a pan, and bring to a boil, then turn down to a simmer until you have a light syrup.

16 Remove the baking sheet from the oven, turn out the loaves onto a wire rack. and while still warm, brush the tops with the rum glaze.

Panettone

The famous Italian Christmas bread should be light, buttery, and aromatic. You can find all sorts of variations, such as chocolate or coffee, but I think the original is the best. Traditionally, to keep the crumb soft, panettone is slightly under-baked, and then suspended upside down until it has cooled. Italian bakeries have special ladder racks for this. Upending the bread stops the dough from collapsing, because it stretches slightly under its own weight, keeping its domed surface. If you can find special paper panettone cases in which to bake the bread, then you can do this at home by threading 2 long skewers through the base of each baked panettone, and then resting the ends on 2 chairs so that the bread hangs upside down between them. If you don't have cases, you will need to grease and line 2 deep 4½ to 5½-inch pans with parchment paper. Obviously you won't be able to suspend the panettones upside down if you bake them in a pan, so they will need to be baked for a little longer to avoid collapsing, but they will still taste beautiful.

A homemade panettone makes a great present, and will keep for a couple of weeks wrapped in parchment paper, inside a freezer bag. Any that is still left over is fantastic in a bread and butter pudding or ice cream (see page 221). It also freezes well, so you can keep one for another time.

Panettone Ferment

Read through the stages of the recipe in advance and plan ahead, because the whole process will take at least a day (if you have nothing much else to do!) or up to 24 hours. For this recipe only, I suggest you use very strong bread flour, as you need its extra strength to carry the richness of the butter through the long fermentation.

STAGE 1:
50g cool water
65g very strong white bread flour
20g compressed fresh yeast
15g superfine sugar

The quantities here are too small for a dough hook, so you need to whisk them together by hand, but do so in your mixer bowl, as you will need to use the mixer when you add the next stage of ingredients.

Put the water into the bowl, add the flour, and break up the compressed fresh yeast on top. Add the superfine sugar, and whisk the ingredients together for about a minute, until well mixed. Cover with a large freezer bag, and leave for 2 hours to ferment.

STAGE 2:
45g cool water
95g very strong white bread flour
30g superfine sugar
25g cold unsalted butter

Add the water to the ferment in your mixer bowl, then the flour and sugar. Break up the pieces of butter and scatter on top. Mix well for a minute on the slowest speed for 4 minutes. Scrape the sides of the bowl and leave to rest, covered as before, for another 2 hours.

STAGE 3:
50g cool water
125g very strong white bread flour
45g superfine sugar
25g cold unsalted butter

Add the water to the ferment in your mixer bowl, then the flour and sugar. Break up the pieces of butter and scatter on top. Mix on the slowest speed for about 6 minutes, until the dough is soft and shiny. Again scrape the sides of the bowl, and leave to rest, covered as before, for 2 hours.

1 While the dough is resting, place the cold butter between two sheets of parchment paper, and bash it with the end of a rolling pin to soften and break it up into small pieces. Put into a bowl and combine with the confectioners' sugar, using a wooden spoon. Put in the fridge until needed.

2 Add the egg yolks to the dough in your mixer bowl, then the flour, salt, and sugar, and mix on slow speed for 10 minutes until soft and shiny. You need to keep this long, slow mixing, so that the dough doesn't warm up. Take the buttered confectioners' sugar mixture from the fridge, and start adding it a little at a time, still with the mixer on slow speed. Continue to mix for an additional 10 to 12 minutes, or until all the butter and sugar has been incorporated, and the dough is light, shiny, and soft.

3 Now it is time to add the vanilla and fruit. Split the vanilla bean, and scrape the seeds into a bowl. Add the orange zest, candied peel, golden raisins and rum, and stir to combine.

4 Add to the dough, and mix for no longer than 30 to 40 seconds on the slowest speed, taking care not to break up the fruit and peel, then turn off the mixer.

5 Lightly flour the work surface, and also a clean bowl. Use a scraper to turn out the dough onto the work surface.

6 Stretch the dough and fold it over itself a few times, then form it into a ball following steps 20 to 23 on pages 50 to 52, and leave to rest for about 45 minutes, until just under double in size (see page 27).

7 Turn out the dough again onto a lightly floured work surface, and re-form into a ball as above, then return it to the bowl, and cover as before. Leave to rest for an additional 30 minutes.

8 Meanwhile, if using cake pans, grease them with butter, and line them with parchment paper, so that it stands about 4 inches above the rim of each pan.

9 Turn out the dough, and divide in half, then reshape each piece into a ball again, as above.

10 Place each ball into a prepared case or pan. Leave to rise for about 6 to 10 hours (the dough is very rich, so it could take a long time), until the dough has risen to just above the cases or pans.

11 Preheat the oven to 375°F, and place the panettones in their cases or pans on a baking sheet.

12 Beat the egg and milk for the glaze in a bowl, and brush the tops of the panettones.

MAKES 2 (800G) PANETTONES

200g cold unsalted butter
75g confectioners' sugar
5 large egg yolks
250g very strong bread flour
10g fine sea salt
60g superfine sugar

For the fruit:
1 vanilla bean
zest of 2 oranges
400g candied peel
250g golden raisins
1 tablespoon rum

For the glaze:
1 egg
2 tablespoons milk

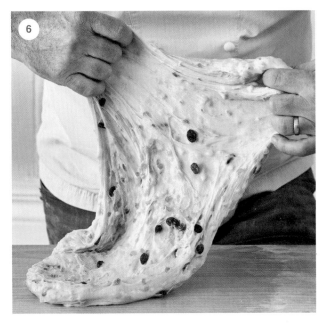

13 Put the baking sheet into the oven, turn down the heat to 350°F, and bake for 10 minutes. Turn the temperature down again to between 350°F and 325°F and bake for an additional 35 minutes if using cases, or for about 40 to 45 minutes if using pans, until the top is domed and golden brown. If using pans, you will see that the panettone is shrinking away from the sides slightly.

14 If you are using panettone cases, toward the end of the baking time, have four long skewers ready.

15 Remove the panettones from the oven, and if using pans, leave to cool before turning out.

16 If using cases, insert one skewer through the panettone, about 1¼ inches from the base, and a quarter of the way across, then insert a second skewer parallel to it. Do the same with the other panettone.

17 Use the ends of the skewers to suspend the panettones upside down between two chairs—or anything that is taller than the panettone (this process helps to keep their domed shape). Leave to cool and stretch for at least an hour, before setting them on a wire rack to cool completely.

Flatbreads and batters

You might ask why I am including flatbreads and batters in this book, as flatbreads have very little crumb; there is an idea that a batter is just a mixture for making pancakes. However, a batter is only a different kind of dough that is used to achieve a particular texture—from the unique, waxy interior of crumpets, to the soft crumbliness of cornbread. In a bread such as the Seeded loaf on page 203, using a batter enables you to keep the crumb moist and cake-like, despite being quite compact, due to the density of seeds, which could otherwise create a dry texture. The particular batter used for this loaf also allows the bread to be both gluten-free and vegan.

You can make great flatbreads with a fantastic texture and flavour using flour milled from different grains and pulses, such as rice, corn and chickpea.

I am always being asked for gluten-free recipes, and whereas the reality is you can't make a sourdough or a baguette without strong bread flour, you can make great flatbreads with fantastic texture and flavor, using flour milled from different grains and legumes, such as rice, corn, and chickpeas. They can be thin and crispy on the outside, or slightly thicker and softer—it is up to you, though the quality of the crumb is still important, and you don't want to make them too thick, or you risk losing the light, digestible texture.

The bonus is that all the recipes in this chapter are very straightforward and easy to make, as they don't need long resting times and need no rising.

The flatbreads can all be cooked quickly in a skillet, but an alternative idea is to bake them in the oven, on top of a bed of washed and scrubbed pebbles, which produce dimples in the dough as it puffs up—though it will deflate when it comes out of the oven. I put the pebbles into a terracotta dish, but you could use a baking pan. As with a bread stone, put the dish or pan, and pebbles into the oven for a good hour before baking (you can do this at 200°F before turning up the heat to 450°F), so that the pebbles really heat through before you put your breads on top.

Socca

These are gluten-free flatbreads made with chickpea flour. They are a classic street food in and around Nice, where vendors cook them on a huge grill, then cut them up, sprinkle them with rosemary and pepper, and hand them to you in paper bags, still warm.

Socca make great wraps for salad, or try them as nibbles, with a glass of chilled rosé, some olives, and a quick chickpea purée, made by briefly pulsing a can of well-drained chickpeas with 2 garlic cloves in a blender, until you have a stiff paste (you can add a chopped chile if you want to give it some heat), then adding the juice of a lemon and pulsing again, before slowly adding up to 250g of extra virgin olive oil, until the paste is quite loose.

You could use green pea flour (see page 194), or buckwheat flour for the batter, instead of chickpea flour as other gluten-free options. And instead of herbs, you could add some chopped olives or sun-dried tomatoes.

A trick from my native Brittany for greasing the pans lightly and easily, is to cut a potato in half, spear it with a fork so that it is cut-side down, then dip it into a shallow bowl of oil, and rub it all over the surface.

MAKES 4 LARGE OR 12 SMALL FLATBREADS
(depending on the size of your pan)

150g chickpea flour
5g fine sea salt
30g extra virgin olive oil
300g warm water
freshly ground black pepper, to taste
1 tablespoon chopped fresh oregano, thyme, or rosemary
light olive oil, for greasing the pan

---

1 Combine the flour with the salt in a mixing bowl.

2 Add the oil and water, and mix well, then add the pepper and herbs, and leave to rest for 15 minutes.

3 Meanwhile, lightly grease a skillet with olive oil, and heat it up, then ladle in some of the mixture, and swirl it around so that it is spread evenly over the base of the pan, in a thin layer, like a *crêpe*.

4 Cook for about 1 to 2 minutes on each side, until lightly colored, and repeat with the rest of the mixture.

Whole-wheat and yogurt flatbreads

In India, the flatbreads are traditionally rolled out using beautiful tapered rolling pins like the one in the photograph, which I found in an antique shop. They make a great accompaniment to a curry, in which case you can add some spice, such as cumin, to the flour. These are made with 50:50 all-purpose white and whole-wheat flour, but you can use all white flour if you prefer.

In India, half an onion is traditionally used to spread the ghee or vegetable oil over the pan, but I don't like the flavor of onion in bread, so I stick to my Breton method of using half a potato! The breads will puff up as they cook, so you can split them in half, like a pita bread, giving yourself a pocket to fill with whatever ingredients you like. My favorite filling is not in the least bit Indian: a little salad made with feta, olives, and fresh mint, with plenty of good extra virgin olive oil drizzled over the top.

MAKES 8 FLATBREADS

250g all-purpose flour
250g whole-wheat flour, plus extra for dusting
15g compressed fresh yeast
10g fine sea salt
150g goat milk yogurt
1 tablespoon honey
a little ghee or vegetable oil, for greasing the pan

1 Mix the flours together in a large bowl. Break up the compressed fresh yeast on one side of the bowl, and add the salt on the other side. Lightly rub the yeast into the flour between the flats of your hands, as if you were washing your hands.

2 Add the yogurt and honey, and mix together for about 3 to 5 minutes, until you have a fairly firm dough.

3 Cover with a baking cloth, or a large freezer bag, and rest for at least 30 minutes.

4 Turn out onto a lightly floured surface, and divide into 8 equal pieces. Roll out each piece to a size that will fit in your skillet.

5 Lightly grease the pan with ghee or oil, and put over medium heat, then cook the flatbreads, one at a time, for about 1 to 2 minutes, until golden on each side. (Keep cooked ones warm wrapped inside a clean dish towel as you go).

Green pea flatbread

This is a vegan flatbread with a beautiful vibrant color and surprisingly pea-flavored crumb, for which I have to give full credit to cook and food writer Jenny Chandler. Jenny regularly teaches at the Bertinet Kitchen and her latest book, *Pulse*, is all about her favorite subject: legumes. She is so passionate about them, that she was invited by the United Nations FAO (Food and Agriculture Organization), to be their European Special Ambassador for the 2016 International Year of Pulses! The green pea flour we use is from Hodmedod's, in Suffolk, who specialize in grains and legumes grown on British farms, as well as the flours that can be milled from them. Americans can source it online.

In this recipe I have to use the word I normally hate in relation to bread: kneading, which you simply have to do with a tight, firm dough like this!

MAKES 4 FLATBREADS

120g green pea flour
80g all-purpose flour, plus
  extra for dusting
5g fine sea salt
10g baking powder
100g water
a little vegetable oil, for
  greasing the pan

1 Combine the dry ingredients in a mixing bowl. Add the water, and mix well into a firm dough.

2 Turn the dough out onto the work surface (don't flour it first), and knead for 3 to 4 minutes, until smooth.

3 Shape the dough into a ball, and put back into the bowl. Cover with a baking cloth, or a large freezer bag, and leave to rest for 15 to 20 minutes.

4 Divide into 4 equal pieces, and reshape each one into a ball. Roll out each one thinly on a lightly floured work surface.

5 Lightly grease a skillet with oil, put over medium heat, and cook the flatbreads one at a time for about 1 to 2 minutes on each side until golden.

Cornbread with Manchego cheese and chorizo

I had never been much of a fan of cornbread, as I usually found it to be quite dry and dense, but then, on a family holiday in Miami, some friends took us to a small local restaurant, where they served cornbread in a skillet, still warm from the oven, with grilled chicken, and I was converted. In different regions of America, everyone has an opinion on what makes the best cornbread, and in general, Northern recipes tend to be sweeter than Southern ones. I like to put in just a little maple syrup, which helps the flavor, but the bread stays savory, and I have added my own twist with some pieces of Manchego cheese and smoky chorizo.

1 Preheat the oven to 400°F, and put in a skillet to heat up.

2 Heat a little vegetable oil in a pan, and fry the chorizo briefly until just colored, then lift out, drain on paper towels, and set aside. If you like, you can keep the oil, which will be flavored by the chorizo, to glaze the cornbread when it comes out of the oven.

3 Melt the butter in a small pan, then remove from the heat.

4 Combine the cornmeal, flour, salt, and baking powder in a mixing bowl. Lightly whisk in the maple syrup, milk, buttermilk, two-thirds of the melted butter, and the eggs—you want the mixing to be as brief as possible—to form a thick batter. Fold in the grated cheese and fried chorizo.

5 Remove the skillet from the oven, and brush the inside all over with the rest of the melted butter.

6 Pour in the batter and put into the oven. Turn the temperature down to 375°F, and bake for 10 minutes, then turn the temperature down again to 350°F for an additional 20 minutes.

7 To check that the cornbread is ready, insert a skewer, or the point of a small sharp knife into the center. It should come out clean. If you wish, glaze the top by brushing it with a little of the reserved chorizo oil.

8 Serve the cornbread warm, straight from the skillet, so everyone can break off a piece.

MAKES AN 8 TO 8½-INCH CORNBREAD, ENOUGH FOR 6 SERVINGS

a little vegetable oil
100g cured chorizo (whether hot or mild is up to you), cut into small dice
100g unsalted butter
150g coarse cornmeal
75g all-purpose flour
10g fine sea salt
2 teaspoons baking powder
25g maple syrup
40g whole milk
100g buttermilk
2 extra-large eggs
100g Manchego cheese, grated

Crumpets

I never saw crumpets in France, but ever since I came to England I have loved them, along with the muffins on page 134. There is something fantastically comforting about a toasted crumpet, spread with butter that melts into the little holes, either for breakfast or in the afternoon.

You will need metal crumpet rings, and a wide, heavy-bottomed skillet, big enough to cook four or five at a time. The knack is to get the pan hot first with a good coating of oil—not so hot that you fry the crumpets, but hot enough to cook them all the way through slowly, without burning the undersides. I usually manage to burn the first one! So cook one by itself first, for a test run. You can always have the oven on at 400°F, and then pop them in for a few minutes to finish off.

**MAKES ABOUT
20 CRUMPETS**

250g all-purpose flour (gluten-free is fine)
10g compressed fresh yeast
250g whole milk
20g honey
125g water
pinch of fine sea salt
10g malt vinegar
vegetable oil, for greasing the rings and the pan

1 Put the flour in a large bowl. Break up the yeast on top and rub into the flour using the flats of your hands—as if you were washing your hands.

2 Add the milk and honey, and mix together to form a thick batter.

3 Cover with a baking cloth, or large freezer bag, and allow to rest for at least 30 minutes, until the batter bubbles up.

4 Warm the water, salt, and vinegar in a small pan, then remove from the heat, stir into the batter, and mix gently. Leave to rest, covered as before, for an additional 20 to 30 minutes.

5 Cook the crumpets in batches. Grease the rings, and coat the base of the pan well with vegetable oil. Put the rings into the pan, and place over a medium–low heat—you want the oil in the pan to be hot, but not sizzling.

6 Use a ladle to fill each ring to just below the rim, and cook for about 10 to 12 minutes, until the crumpets are light golden underneath, but still quite white on top.

7 Leave to cool, and then toast them before eating with butter.

Blueberry and blue corn pancakes

I love the purple color that the blue cornstarch gives to these pancakes, and the way the blueberries pop with flavor when you bite into one. Both cornstarch and rice flour are gluten-free, and I have used almond milk here, but you can use dairy milk if you prefer You need about 100g blueberries to go into the batter as it cooks, but if you buy a big basket, you will have some to serve alongside the pancakes, perhaps with some yogurt.

---

1 Combine the flour, cornstarch, baking powder, and sugar (or honey) in a mixing bowl.

2 Whisk in the melted butter, eggs, almond milk, and sour cream until smooth.

3 Leave the batter to rest in the fridge for 30 minutes. Meanwhile, grease a large skillet or grill pan (or several blini pans) with vegetable oil.

4 When you're ready to cook, heat the pan (or pans) until hot.

5 Ladle a dollop or two of the batter at a time into the pan. Sprinkle a few blueberries into the center, and cook for about a minute on each side. Serve warm, with any remaining blueberries and some yogurt, if you like.

MAKES ABOUT 6 (4-INCH) PANCAKES

125g rice flour
125g blue cornflour
10g baking powder
60g superfine sugar (or honey)
50g unsalted butter, melted
2 extra-large eggs
200g almond milk
100g sour cream
100g blueberries, plus extra to serve
a little vegetable oil, for greasing the pan
plain yogurt, to serve

Seeded loaf

This loaf is vegan and gluten-free. I have used almond milk, so that it is dairy-free too, and as full of nuts and seeds, it is very nutritious, but the important thing is that it is also really tasty, with a crumb that is quite dense, but very moist. Because it contains no flour or yeast, the loaf is made with a batter, rather than a dough. Wrapped in waxed paper, the loaf should last for 3 to 4 days.

MAKES 1 (900G) LOAF

100g blanched hazelnuts
180g rolled gluten-free oats
1 tablespoon baking powder
150g sunflower seeds
100g flaxseeds
2 tablespoons chia seeds
1 teaspoon fine sea salt
1 tablespoon maple syrup
3 tablespoons cold-pressed canola oil
350g almond milk
a little vegetable oil, for greasing the pan

1 Toast the hazelnuts in a dry skillet until just colored, then chop by hand into small pieces, or pulse briefly in a blender. Tip into a large bowl, and add the oats, baking powder, seeds, and salt, mixing well.

2 In a separate bowl, mix together the maple syrup, canola oil, and the milk. Add to the bowl containing the dry ingredients, and mix well to form a batter.

3 Cover with a baking cloth or a large freezer bag, and leave to rest for 2 hours (or leave overnight in the fridge).

4 When you are ready to bake, preheat the oven to 350°F and grease a 9 x 5-inch loaf pan with vegetable oil.

5 Ladle the batter into the pan, pressing it down gently. Transfer to the preheated oven, and bake for about 30 to 40 minutes, until firm and slightly crisp on top, and a skewer inserted into the center comes out clean.

6 Leave until completely cool before eating—use a sharp knife to slice it.

Pain d'épices

For me, as for most French people, this brings back memories of childhood—coming home from school, and tucking into a slice with a glass of milk. It is a really simple recipe, and is quick and easy to make by hand. The addition of rye flour is traditional, and it gives the crumb both a richness of flavor, and a little acidity. Because the loaf contains a lot of honey, try to find a good one, preferably a single varietal, which will have much more of a distinctive flavor. I found a brilliant fir tree honey that had a unique "green" pine flavor, but orange blossom or heather would also be good.

There is no need to rest the *Pain d'épices* dough. Once baked, keep the loaf wrapped in waxed paper to prevent it from drying out.

MAKES 1 LOAF

350g good honey
40g soft dark brown sugar
125g all-purpose flour
125g rye flour
1 tablespoon pumpkin pie spice (typically ground ginger, nutmeg, cinnamon, allspice and cloves)
1 teaspoon star anise
20g baking powder
2 extra-large eggs
100g whole milk
20g butter, for greasing the pan

1 Preheat the oven to 350°F. Gently heat the honey in a pan with the sugar, stirring until the sugar melts, then remove from the heat.

2 Combine the all-purpose flour, rye flour, pumpkin pie spice, star anise, and baking powder in a bowl.

3 In a separate bowl, beat together the eggs and milk, and then stir in the honey and sugar mixture. Stir this into the dry ingredients to form a batter.

4 Melt the butter in a small pan, and use to brush the inside of a 10-inch long loaf pan.

5 Fill the pan with the batter, transfer to the preheated oven, and bake for 35 minutes, until the top is dark brown, and a skewer inserted into the middle comes out clean.

Cooking with bread

I try never to waste bread: any that is left over can be cut into squares and toasted in the oven to make croûtons, or dried out in the oven and then blitzed in a blender for bread crumbs, or toasted to make *tartines* to serve with drinks. You can also use leftover bread to make gazpacho or Brioche ice cream. And who doesn't like Croque monsieur, the staple of Parisian cafés? Or, if you have a whole loaf that is a day or two old, try the two versions of Pain surprise on pages 216 and 220—one made with tomatoes, prosciutto, and mozzarella for a summer's day, and the other inspired by mountain food for the winter, both of which make a great lunch for family or friends to share.

I particularly love the crab and celeriac toasts served by my good friends, Marty Grant and Richard Knighting (pictured below), at Corkage in Bath, one of my favorite places to go and relax over a great glass of wine and a brilliant selection of small plates. My version of their idea is on page 212. Or for an indulgent afternoon treat, try the salted caramel on page 163, drizzled onto toasted bread.

Gazpacho

The key to this fantastic soup, is of course, ripe, full-flavored tomatoes and lots of good virgin olive oil—and I do mean lots! It is simple to make, but do make it ahead and allow all the flavors to mingle together in the bowl before blitzing it. Perfect for a hot day.

---

1 Roughly chop the tomatoes, retaining all the juice.

2 Tear the bread into pieces and put into a large, wide bowl.

3 Drizzle two-thirds of the extra virgin olive oil, and then the vinegar, over the bread.

4 Add half the basil, and all of the garlic. Squeeze the bread with your fingers, so the garlic is well incorporated.

5 Mix in the tomatoes—with their juice—and the peppers, then add the cucumber. Season with the paprika, and salt and pepper. Stir well, and put the bowl in the fridge for 1 hour.

6 Transfer to a blender, and blend until smooth. Check and adjust the seasoning if necessary. Serve chilled, scattered with the rest of the basil, torn or roughly chopped, and with a swirl of extra virgin olive oil or avocado oil. And bread!

SERVES 8

about 600g ripe tomatoes
3 large slices of bread (or stale baguette is good)
at least 200g extra virgin olive oil
3 tablespoons sherry vinegar or red wine vinegar
handful of basil leaves
3 garlic cloves, crushed
2 red or green peppers, seeded and chopped
1 medium cucumber, pared, halved, seeded, and chopped
large pinch of paprika
sea salt and freshly ground black pepper
a little more extra virgin olive oil, or avocado oil, to serve

Croque monsieur

The best snack in the world—at least if you are French! For me, bread, ham, and cheese is just the greatest combination, any time of the day, and you can turn it into a Croque Madame for brunch, by putting a fried egg on top.

1 Preheat the oven to 400°F while you make the béchamel sauce.

2 Melt the butter in a heavy-bottomed pan over medium heat, then add the flour, remove from the heat, and whisk briskly, until you have a paste that comes away cleanly from the edges of the pan.

3 Whisk in the milk a little at a time, to avoid any lumps.

4 Return to the stovetop, and cook over medium-low heat, until the sauce begins to bubble. Continue to cook for an additional minute, season to taste, and add the nutmeg. Remove from the heat.

5 Leave the béchamel to cool, then spread a little over each slice of bread, add a slice of ham to half the bread, and then sandwich with the remaining bread.

6 Lay the sandwiches on a baking sheet, spread a thick layer of béchamel over the top of each one, and then sprinkle with the cheese.

7 Put into the preheated oven for about 12 minutes, until the cheese is melted and golden.

MAKES 4 TOASTED SANDWICHES

8 slices of *Pain de mie* (see page 137)
4 thick slices of ham
about 4 tablespoons grated Gruyère cheese

For the béchamel sauce:
50g unsalted butter
40g all-purpose flour
300g whole milk
sea salt and freshly ground black pepper
a little freshly grated nutmeg

Tartines

For the French, a *tartine* is simply a slice of bread. Most usually it has come to mean the equivalent of the Italian bruschetta: a toasted slice of good sourdough or other rustic bread, topped with whatever you like. For bruschetta-style *tartines*, I like to make a selection of toppings which can be as simple as a little crème fraîche topped with smoked salmon, a chunky pesto, or the combination of crab and celeriac in the recipe below. I also like to crush fava beans or peas—or both —with some chopped mint and Parmesan, and bind all together with good extra virgin olive oil. Or I will wrap some small beets in foil, and bake them whole in the oven (or you can use ready-cooked beets), then peel them and pulse briefly in a blender, so that they still have plenty of texture, season with salt and pepper, then cool and mix in a little crème fraîche.

However, you can also make something quite substantial by layering up ingredients on your bread, and baking the slices in the oven, as in the recipe for Baked Belgian endive and ham on page 215.

Crab

I like to make fresh mayonnaise for this, but you can use about 150g of a good, thick, bought one if you prefer.

1 To make the mayonnaise, put the egg yolks in a wide bowl, whisk in the mustard, then begin to dribble in the vegetable oil, a drop at a time at first, whisking all the time. As the mayonnaise starts to thicken, you can increase the addition of the oil to a steady stream.

2 When the vegetable oil is all incorporated, start to add the olive oil, whisking continuously, until you have a thick mayonnaise (the more oil you add, the thicker it will be). Season it well.

3 Stir the brown crabmeat into the mayonnaise, then stir in the celeriac. Add the white crabmeat, and mix in lemon juice to taste. Season again if necessary. Finally mix in the chopped chives.

4 Put into the fridge to chill for 30 minutes before spooning the mixture onto the toasted bread.

SERVES 4

50g brown crabmeat and
  400g white crabmeat
1 small celeriac (celery root),
  peeled and grated
lemon juice, to taste
small bunch of chives, finely
  chopped
sea salt and freshly ground
  black pepper

For the mayonnaise:
2 egg yolks
1 teaspoon Dijon mustard
about 100g vegetable oil
50g good olive oil
sea salt and freshly ground
  black pepper

4 large slices of sourdough, or
  rustic bread of your choice,
  toasted

Baked Belgian endive and ham

This makes a great lunch with a crisp green salad, tossed in a sharp vinaigrette to cut through the richness of the *tartine*.

---

1 Preheat the oven to 375°F while you make the béchamel sauce.

2 Place the slices of bread on a parchment paper-lined baking sheet and spread a little béchamel on each one.

3 Lay a slice of ham on top.

4 Roughly chop the Belgian endive, then mix into the remaining béchamel, and spoon on top of the ham, making sure you cover it well.

5 Sprinkle the cheese over the top.

6 Season, and if you like, sprinkle a little nutmeg over each *tartine*.

7 Put into the preheated oven and bake for about 12 to 15 minutes, until the cheese is brown and bubbling, and the sourdough is crisp around the edges.

SERVES 4

300g béchamel sauce (see page 211)
4 slices of sourdough bread
4 slices of good cooked ham
2 heads of Belgian endive, trimmed
200g grated Emmental or Gruyère cheese
sea salt and freshly ground black pepper
freshly grated nutmeg (optional)

Winter pain surprise

This is a play on *Tartiflette*, the seriously rich French "mountain" dish of potatoes, bacon cubes, and cheese, layered up and baked. I have just layered the ingredients between slices of bread instead! It is really tasty, but very filling, so it will serve a lot of people with a good mixed salad, and a sharp chutney to cut through the richness.

olive oil, for greasing
200g bacon in one piece, cut into cubes
1 shallot, finely sliced
1 small leek, finely sliced
250g crème fraîche
2 whole eggs
sea salt and freshly ground black pepper
freshly ground nutmeg, to taste
1 large country or sourdough loaf
2 medium potatoes, cooked and thickly sliced
1 Reblochon (or ripe Camembert) cheese, thickly sliced

1 Preheat the oven to 375°F. Very lightly grease a pan with olive oil, put in the bacon cubes, and sauté until colored, then add the chopped shallot. Cook until softened, but not colored, then add the leek. Stir together, and remove from the heat—you want the leeks to keep their color, so don't carry on cooking them.

2 Stir the crème fraîche and eggs together in a bowl, and season with salt, pepper, and nutmeg. Don't overmix: keep the mixture a little lumpy.

3 Put the bread on a sheet of parchment paper, large enough to wrap the bread. Slice into the bread, but not all the way through. You need to cut deep enough into the bread to be able to open out the loaf and fill between the "slices," while leaving the loaf connected at the base.

5 Stuff a slice of potato into each slot in the bread and follow with some of the bacon cubes, shallots, and leeks.

6 Use the parchment paper to lift the bread onto a baking pan. Spoon some of the cream and egg mixture into each slot, so that the bread absorbs as much as possible.

7 Finally insert the slices of cheese. Enclose the loaf fully in the parchment paper, and then wrap it in foil to make a tight parcel.

8 Put the wrapped bread into the preheated oven and bake for 30 to 40 minutes, then remove the baking pan, and open the top of the foil and parchment paper. Return to the oven until the top of the bread and its filling have turned golden brown.

9 Remove from the oven and let everyone help themselves to chunks.

Summer pain surprise

This is made in the same way as the winter version on page 216, but the inspiration was *Pan Bagnat*, the traditional Nice "sandwich," in which the top of a round loaf would be sliced off and some of the crumb hollowed out, mixed with tuna, olives, anchovies, etc. then spooned back in and the "lid" put on top. Later variations are often made with ham and cheese, and sometimes peppers layered up neatly inside the bread "shell," but I thought it would be fun to stuff the ingredients between the slices of a whole loaf, and bake it. We often make this for lunch. and everyone loves it warm, but it is also a great picnic showstopper. You can carry it with you, still in its foil, then just open it up, drizzle with oil and let everyone help themselves. Although I have suggested using prosciutto and mozzarella, which melts very well, I always associate *pain surprise* with Provence, as I like to make it when I am there on holiday with the family, but using local cured ham and cheese instead.

SERVES 10 TO 12

1 large sourdough loaf
6 slices of prosciutto, torn into pieces
1 to 2 whole buffalo mozzarellas, sliced
2 to 3 large ripe tomatoes, sliced
1 shallot or small red onion, sliced wafer thin
1 garlic clove, sliced wafer thin
a handful of mixed herbs, such as rosemary, thyme, and basil
extra virgin olive oil
1 tablespoon capers (optional)

---

1 Preheat the oven to 375°F.

2 Put the loaf of bread on a sheet of parchment paper large enough to wrap the bread. Slice into the bread, but not all the way through, leaving the loaf connected at the base. You need to cut deep enough into the bread to be able to open out the loaf, and fill between the "slices" (see previous page).

3 Stuff each slot in the bread with the ham, mozzarella, tomatoes, shallot, garlic, and herbs. Season well.

4 Use the parchment paper to lift the bread onto a baking pan. Drizzle plenty of olive oil over the loaf, focusing on the crevices, and add a few capers if you like.

5 Enclose the loaf fully in the parchment paper, and then wrap it in foil to make a tight parcel.

6 Put the wrapped bread into the preheated oven, and bake for 15 minutes, then remove the pan, and open the top of the foil and parchment paper. Return to the oven for an additional 5 minutes, until golden brown on top.

7 Remove from the oven and let everyone help themselves to chunks.

Brioche ice cream

The thought of ice cream made with bread never really appealed to me, but one day I decided to experiment by adding some leftover slices of fruited brioche to a simple homemade vanilla ice cream that I was churning, and I loved the result. You can of course use any bread you like. Panettone (see page 181) is especially good.

SERVES 8 TO 10

about 200g stale brioche made with fruit or chocolate chips
1 tablespoon rum, or your favorite tipple
8 egg yolks
100g superfine sugar
250g heavy cream
250g whole milk
1 vanilla bean, split

1 Mix the bread and the rum in a bowl, and leave to soak for at least an hour at room temperature.

2 Whisk the egg yolks and sugar in a separate bowl.

3 Pour the cream and milk into a pan, and add the split vanilla bean, scraping in the seeds. Put over a medium-low heat, and take the pan off the heat when the mixture just begins to simmer. Remove the vanilla bean.

4 Pour half of the hot vanilla cream over the egg mixture, and whisk well, then whisk in the rest.

5 Return the mixture to the pan, return to the heat, and stir continuously in a figure eight motion with a wooden spoon, until you have a custard that is thick enough to coat the back of the spoon, and if you draw a line through it with the tip of a knife, it won't disappear.

6 Stir in the brioche and rum. Leave the custard to cool a little first if you are using brioche studded with chocolate, otherwise it will melt too much.

7 Allow to cool completely before churning in an ice-cream maker.

Index

Acknowledgments

As is always the case, getting a book out of my head and onto the shelves requires a great team effort and there are a host of people without whom it would not be possible. I owe a huge debt of thanks to Kyle Cathie for making this her swansong, to Sheila Keating whose patience and talent is what turns my musings into beautiful and instructive text and to Jean for the beautiful images and his delightful and ubiquitous Frenchness!

To Dimitri for the amazing portrait; you are a genius and I love your work, to Vicky, Tina, Tabitha, Nic, Gemma and the team at Kyle Books for all your input and to Jen, my head of kitchen, Spud and Lisa for all the prep, baking and washing up.

To Jenny Chandler for your help, support and brilliant teaching at the school over the years and for allowing me to use your Green pea flatbread recipe, to Angela and Nathan for your kinds words and your friendship and to Pierre Koffmann: you were one of the earliest influences on my career and to be able to share a drink and some bread with you now is a real treat.

To Emily at Wessex Mill for your amazing flour and posing for the book. Lydia and Toby Whatley at Toad's Mill: I am so pleased to see your business growing—your flour is really special, to the lovely people at Hodmedods for the green pea and chickpea flours, to Laura at The Italian Food Hall for the props and to Marty and Richard at Corkage in Bath for the inspiration for the crab recipe and for hosting a shoot for us.

Finally to Jo (Mrs Bun), love and thanks as always for all your support and keeping the ship in a straight line; my awesome kids Jack, Tom and Lola, chief tasters and critics; and to Carrie, Sarah and Kelly (the gannets!!) at Bertinet HQ.

Thank you all!